Food Truck Business

The Complete Guide to Starting With Confidence

(A Practical Handbook to Guide You Launching & Successfully Getting Your Food Business)

Terry Shephard

Published By **Kate Sanders**

Terry Shephard

All Rights Reserved

Food Truck Business: The Complete Guide to Starting With Confidence (A Practical Handbook to Guide You Launching & Successfully Getting Your Food Business)

ISBN 978-1-7753927-8-1

No part of this guidebook shall be reproduced in any form without permission in writing from the publisher except in the case of brief quotations embodied in critical articles or reviews.

Legal & Disclaimer

The information contained in this book is not designed to replace or take the place of any form of medicine or professional medical advice. The information in this book has been provided for educational & entertainment purposes only.

The information contained in this book has been compiled from sources deemed reliable, and it is accurate to the best of the Author's knowledge; however, the Author cannot guarantee its accuracy and validity and cannot be held liable for any errors or omissions. Changes are periodically made to this book. You must consult your doctor or get professional medical advice before using any of the suggested remedies, techniques, or information in this book.

Upon using the information contained in this book, you agree to hold harmless the Author from and against any damages, costs, and expenses, including any legal fees potentially resulting from the application of any of the information provided by this guide. This disclaimer applies to any damages or injury caused by the use and application, whether directly or indirectly, of any advice or information presented, whether for breach of contract, tort, negligence, personal injury, criminal intent, or under any other cause of action.

You agree to accept all risks of using the information presented inside this book. You need to consult a professional medical practitioner in order to ensure you are both able and healthy enough to participate in this program.

Table Of Contents

Chapter 1: The Food Truck Industry 1

Chapter 2: Developing Your Concept 19

Chapter 3: Legalities and Regulations 47

Chapter 4: A Look Back At Food Truck History 69

Chapter 5: How to Locate Food Vehicles 87

Chapter 6: The Location of a Food Truck Purchase 103

Chapter 7: Additional Start-Up Expenses For Restaurants To Consider 116

Chapter 8: The Communications Plan For A Brand 135

Chapter 9: Local and Herbal Food 149

Chapter 10: The Food Truck Industry ... 155

Chapter 11: Market Research and Concept Development 169

Chapter 1: The Food Truck Industry

Growth and Trends

The meals truck corporation has skilled great growth and witnessed numerous key developments, reworking it from a niche idea to a dynamic and influential segment of the food provider organization Understanding the elements riding this increase and the persevering with tendencies within the business enterprise offers treasured insights for marketers and stakeholders.

1. Historical Growth and Emergence

Early Adoption: The food truck enterprise's boom may be traced once more to the late 20th century, with the emergence of connoisseur food motors hard traditional notions of road meals.

Economic Resilience: The agency showcased resilience during economic downturns, supplying an low cost eating opportunity for the duration of difficult instances.

Global Expansion: From its roots inside the United States, the food truck phenomenon has unfold globally, adapting to numerous cultures and culinary landscapes.

2. Entrepreneurial Opportunities

Lower Entry Barriers: The quite decrease startup costs in assessment to standard ingesting locations have made food vehicles an attractive choice for aspiring marketers.

Innovation Incubators: The upward push of meals truck incubators and assist networks has facilitated entrepreneurship, imparting steering and property to beginners.

3. Economic Impact

Local Economic Contributions: Food automobiles contribute notably to neighborhood economies thru producing income, growing jobs, and supporting different groups in their operational regions.

Job Creation: The company has end up a deliver of employment, each at once (cooks, drivers) and not at once (supply chain, occasion coordinators).

four. Technological Integration

Mobile Apps and Online Ordering: Food motors have embraced generation with the adoption of cell apps, permitting customers to music locations and area orders on line.

Data Analytics: Analyzing client records allows meals truck operators optimize menus, understand possibilities, and enhance fundamental client revel in.

five. Culinary Innovation

Gourmet and Fusion Cuisine: Food motors are recounted for pushing culinary limitations, presenting gourmand and fusion delicacies that caters to evolving consumer tastes.

Specialty Offerings: Unique and specialized menu devices, often stimulated thru international culinary tendencies, make a contribution to the industry's enchantment.

6. Health-Conscious Menus

Demand for Healthier Options: Consumers are an increasing number of searching out extra healthy food choices, essential food trucks to incorporate easy, natural, and nutritious materials into their menus.

Dietary Accommodations: Food motors are adapting to dietary developments, offering vegetarian, vegan, gluten-unfastened, and distinctive specialized options.

7. Sustainability Practices

Eco-Friendly Initiatives: Many food vans are adopting sustainable practices, which encompass using inexperienced packaging, domestically sourced elements, and electricity-inexperienced operations.

Community and Environmental Impact: Emphasis on sustainability no longer nice aligns with purchaser values however additionally clearly contributes to the environment and nearby groups.

eight. Collaborations and Pop-Up Events

Collaborative Partnerships: Food vehicles often collaborate with other businesses, breweries, or activities to make bigger their acquire and offer precise studies.

Participation in Food Festivals: Engaging in pop-up activities and food festivals permits food cars connect to a broader target market and check new menu items.

9. Social Media Marketing

Promotion and Engagement: Social media platforms play a pivotal function in advertising and advertising and marketing meals cars, allowing them to hook up with clients, assemble logo popularity, and announce locations in actual-time.

Digital Community Building: Establishing a virtual network through social media fosters customer loyalty and gives a platform for direct conversation.

10. Challenges and Opportunities

Market Saturation: Some regions can also moreover moreover face stressful conditions due to marketplace saturation, emphasizing the need for differentiation and strategic centered on of region of interest markets.

Regulatory Landscape: Navigating and adapting to severa and evolving rules remains a challenge however also gives possibilities for advocacy and shaping favorable environments.

11. Future Outlook

Technological Advancements: The corporation is anticipated to combine rising generation like AI and automation, improving operational overall performance and customer service.

Global Expansion and Cultural Exchange: Continued globalization of food truck actions will make a contribution to the change of culinary affects and trends.

Sustainability as a Core Value: Sustainability practices are likely to emerge as even extra essential to the enterprise, pushed thru the use of growing client awareness and call for for inexperienced alternatives.

Resilience Post-Pandemic: The commercial enterprise employer's functionality to innovate and adapt at some stage in the COVID-19 pandemic highlights its resilience, with prolonged-time period results shaping new operational strategies.

The boom and traits in the meals truck enterprise underscore its adaptability, innovation, and cultural effect. Entrepreneurs and stakeholders within the industry need to stay aware about evolving consumer options, technological upgrades, and sustainability practices to navigate disturbing situations and capitalize on growing possibilities on this dynamic market.

Market Analysis

1. Executive Summary

The food truck organization has witnessed outstanding increase globally, offering a worthwhile opportunity for entrepreneurs to go into the market.

This market analysis dreams to provide insights into client developments, regulatory troubles, and technological improvements to tell the strategic positioning of a cutting-edge food truck agency.

2. Industry Overview

Market Size and Growth: The food truck enterprise has professional sturdy growth, pushed by using manner of patron call for for unique and reachable eating reviews.

Market length estimates imply a multi-billion-dollar organisation, with non-stop boom projected within the coming years.

Geographic Presence: Urban areas with excessive foot internet site web site traffic and numerous demographics present top locations for food truck operations.

The international reap of the commercial enterprise organization affords opportunities for severa culinary affects and cultural exchanges.

Competitive Landscape: The industry skills a mixture of hooked up game enthusiasts and innovative novices supplying numerous cuisines.

Collaboration and partnerships with specific corporations contribute to the industry's dynamic nature.

three. Target Market

Demographics: Identify the purpose demographic primarily based mostly on factors in conjunction with age, earnings degree, and life-style possibilities.

Tailor the food truck concept to attraction to the unique tastes and alternatives of the selected demographic.

Consumer Trends: Address the call for for comfort, fitness-conscious picks, and particular eating reports.

Leverage consumer trends to create a menu that aligns with evolving opportunities.

4. Market Segmentation

Cuisine-Specific Trucks: Consider specializing in a selected delicacies or presenting a totally precise fusion idea to aim place of interest markets.

Evaluate the community culinary panorama to become privy to underserved niches.

Function-Specific Trucks: Explore opportunities in catering for sports activities, weddings, and personal capabilities to diversify profits streams.

Customize menus and offerings based totally totally on the shape of event.

Specialized Concepts Evaluate the feasibility of dessert or beverage-centered standards to provide specific services.

Stay attuned to growing culinary traits for idea.

five. Regulatory Landscape

Licensing and Permits: Understand nearby licensing necessities and strong the crucial permits for meals truck operations.

Establish easy compliance techniques to navigate the regulatory panorama correctly.

Zoning and Location Regulations: Analyze zoning criminal pointers and region guidelines to apprehend highest pleasant running locations.

Build top notch relationships with neighborhood authorities to facilitate clean operations.

6. Technological Integration

Mobile Apps and Online Presence: Develop someone-excellent cellular app for vicinity tracking, on line ordering, and client engagement.

Leverage social media systems to construct logo focus and communicate with customers.

Data Analytics: Implement information analytics system to analyze consumer options, track income tendencies, and optimize the menu.

Utilize generation for operational overall performance and to enhance the general purchaser revel in.

7. SWOT Analysis

Strengths

Flexibility and mobility, bearing in mind strategic positioning in excessive-web page traffic areas.

Ability to comply fast to changing patron possibilities and culinary tendencies.

Weaknesses

Vulnerability to climate situations, impacting outside operations.

Fewer assets and area than standard ingesting places.

Opportunities

Collaboration with neighborhood agencies and participation in sports activities to expand reach.

Integration of sustainable practices to appeal to environmentally conscious customers.

Threats

Market saturation in remarkable regions, requiring differentiation strategies.

Regulatory demanding conditions and converting felony necessities impacting operations.

8. Marketing and Branding

Branding Strategy: Develop a robust and great logo identification that resonates with the goal demographic.

Emphasize the precise selling proposition (USP) to differentiate the meals truck in a aggressive marketplace.

Social Media Marketing: Utilize social media structures for selling, engagement, and actual-time communique with customers.

Implement modern and visually appealing content fabric to reveal off menu gadgets.

9. Financial Projections

Startup Costs: Outline the initial investment required for acquiring or retrofitting a food truck, allows, licenses, and device.

Consider ongoing operational expenses, which embody components, gasoline, and protection.

Revenue Projections: Project sales based on every day income estimates, considering seasonal versions.

Explore capability revenue streams which encompass catering offerings and partnerships.

10. Conclusion

The meals truck business enterprise offers promising possibilities for entrepreneurial fulfillment, provided a strategic technique is taken.

Adapting to client tendencies, navigating regulatory stressful conditions, and leveraging technology might be key to the achievement of the meals truck commercial organisation.

This complete marketplace analysis serves as a foundation for growing a robust organisation technique, guiding selections related to idea development, vicinity preference, advertising and marketing and advertising and advertising, and operational efficiency for the ability food truck enterprise organisation.

Identifying Target Audience

Identifying the target market for a food truck business organisation is a essential step in developing a a fulfillment advertising and advertising technique and tailoring the culinary offerings to meet precise patron goals.

These are a few tips you may have a look at to grow to be aware of the goal market to your meals truck enterprise.

1. Conduct Market Research

Local Demographics: Analyze the demographic composition of the vicinity in which the meals truck plans to operate. Consider factors together with age, profits ranges, career, and cultural range.

Competitor Analysis: Study gift food truck competitors and traditional restaurants in the place. Understand their client base and select out capability gaps within the market.

Event Attendance: If making plans to participate in events or festivals, studies the demographics of attendees. Tailor the menu to in shape the tastes and alternatives of the occasion-goers.

2. Define Your Cuisine and Concept

Specialized Cuisine: If the food truck focuses on a specific cuisine, discover the purpose marketplace that has an affinity for that kind of meals. Consider cultural and close by alternatives.

Conceptual Theme: If the food truck has a totally precise concern or idea, understand the demographic that resonates with that trouble. For example, a food truck with a focal point on sustainable practices can also lure environmentally conscious customers.

3. Leverage Social Media Insights

Social Media Analytics: Utilize social media structures to accumulate insights into the demographics of your contemporary purpose marketplace. Analyze facts which encompass age, area, and pastimes to recognize who engages together with your content material.

Engagement and Feedback: Monitor comments, likes, and stocks on social media to gauge target market engagement. Pay interest to the remarks and alternatives expressed with the aid of enthusiasts.

4. Collect Customer Feedback:

Surveys and Feedback Forms: Implement customer surveys or remarks office work to accumulate records without delay out of your purchasers. Inquire approximately their opportunities, favourite menu gadgets, and demographic records.

In-Person Interactions: Engage with clients for the duration of company hours to gather informal remarks. Conversations can provide valuable insights into consumer opportunities and backgrounds.

Chapter 2: Developing Your Concept

Choosing a Niche

Selecting a gap is a pivotal selection even as beginning a food truck organisation. It defines your culinary identification, aim market, and units the volume for fulfillment.

The following are some steps to take when deciding on a niche that aligns at the aspect of your passion, market call for, and commercial enterprise dreams.

1. Evaluate Your Passion and Expertise

Identify Your Culinary Passion: Consider the types of delicacies or dishes which you are genuinely obsessed with. Your enthusiasm will pressure your determination to the commercial enterprise.

Leverage Culinary Expertise: Assess your culinary skills and knowledge. If you have were given specialized information in a powerful delicacies or cooking approach, leveraging it could set your meals truck apart.

2. Analyze Market Demand

Research Local Trends: Analyze nearby food tendencies and alternatives. Consider the culinary panorama on your goal vicinity to find out capacity gaps or opportunities.

Assess Competitor Offerings: Study present day food motors and consuming locations within the vicinity. Identify what cuisines are already popular and test out whether or no longer there can be room for differentiation.

Consider Dietary Preferences: Take beneath interest nutritional alternatives and fitness-conscious tendencies. Consider offering alternatives for severa diets, consisting of vegetarian, vegan, gluten-free, or low-carb, primarily based on name for.

three. Identify Your Target Audience

Understand Local Demographics: Analyze the demographics of your target area. Consider factors which includes age, income tiers, and cultural range to tailor your region of hobby to the alternatives of your potential clients.

Identify Your Potential Customer: Make a image of your best customer. Understand their manner of lifestyles, alternatives, and expectancies. Your region of interest must resonate with this purpose market.

4. Explore Unique Concepts

Fusion Cuisine: Explore the potential of mixing precise cuisines to create a very precise fusion concept. Fusion dishes can attraction to a numerous patron base searching out novel culinary studies.

Specialized Offerings: Consider that specialize in a selected form of dish, element, or culinary idea. This may also moreover need to variety from connoisseur burgers and tacos to area of expertise cakes or worldwide road food.

five. Consider Lifestyle and Events

Cater to Daily Lifestyles: Align your niche with the daily sporting events and lifestyles of your target audience. For instance, in case you're running in a commercial organisation district, supplying quick and pleasing lunch alternatives is probably a strategic choice.

Event Catering: Assess the potential for catering at sports, festivals, or private abilties. Tailor your area of hobby to meet the desires of occasion-goers, whether or not or now not it is providing opposition-pleasant substances or catering offerings for unique activities.

6. Evaluate Seasonal Considerations

Seasonal Menu Adjustments: Consider how your area of hobby can adapt to seasonal adjustments. For instance, supplying fresh gadgets at some degree within the summer time or at ease, warm temperature dishes inside the winter can attraction to clients in some unspecified time in the future of the twelve months.

Holiday Specials: Introduce excursion-themed specials or confined-time services. This no longer quality maintains your menu dynamic but additionally capitalizes on seasonal celebrations.

7. Assess Operational Feasibility

Equipment and Space Requirements: Evaluate the machine and region had to execute your chosen location of interest. Ensure that your meals truck is equipped to handle the training and storage necessities of your area of hobby.

Skill and Labor Considerations: Consider the talent set and hard work necessities for your selected location of interest. Ensure which you or your corporation non-public the important culinary abilities to constantly deliver tremendous dishes.

8. Conduct Test Runs and Gather Feedback

Pilot Programs: Before completely committing to an opening, recollect taking walks pilot applications or take a look at activities to gauge purchaser reaction. Use this possibility to refine your menu and operations primarily based totally on actual-time feedback.

Customer Surveys: Gather comments from functionality clients thru surveys or tastings. Understand their opportunities, and be inclined to make adjustments based totally absolutely mostly on their input.

9. Align with Brand Identity

Reflect Your Brand Story: Ensure that your preferred area of interest aligns with the overall logo story and identification of your meals truck. Brand consistency will boom purchaser loyalty and receive as genuine with.

Visual Representation: Consider how your region of interest can be visually represented for your food truck. Eye-catching visuals and branding can enchantment to customers and talk your region of interest efficiently.

10. Be Adaptable and Open to Evolution

Flexibility for Evolution: While choosing a gap is a critical choice, be open to evolution. Stay adaptable to changing traits, client remarks, and developing culinary standards.

Seasonal Menu Changes: Introduce seasonal menu changes or restrained-time specials to hold your offerings glowing and interesting.

This adaptability contributes to the longevity of your meals truck.

Choosing a gap on your food truck corporation requires a cautious balance among non-public passion, marketplace name for, and operational feasibility. By aligning your area of interest at the side of your capabilities, information the options of your target marketplace, and staying adaptable, you put the foundation for a a achievement and specific meals truck task.

Menu Planning and Innovation

Menu planning and innovation are crucial components of a a achievement food truck organisation. Crafting a well-notion-out menu that balances client opportunities, culinary creativity, and operational usual overall performance can set your meals truck apart in a competitive market.

Follow the following steps to grasp the artwork of menu making plans and innovation:

1. Understand Your Target Audience

Demographic Analysis: Conduct an in depth assessment of the demographics for your target place. Understand the age agencies, options, and cultural affects that form the tastes of your capacity clients.

Customer Preferences: Gather comments from your target audience via surveys, social media interactions, and tastings. Identify well-known flavors, dietary alternatives, and the sorts of dishes that resonate with them.

2. Craft a Signature Dish

Create a Culinary Identity: Develop a signature dish that represents your food truck's culinary identity. This standout item can come to be a focus of your advertising efforts and enchantment to customers seeking a completely particular revel in.

Highlight Unique Ingredients: Feature precise and regionally sourced substances in your signature dish. This now not best provides a extraordinary taste but moreover aligns with the growing call for for smooth and sustainable meals alternatives.

three. Balance Familiarity and Innovation

Classic Favorites: Include acquainted and conventional favorites on your menu to cater to a full-size patron base. Classics provide a enjoy of comfort and are regularly well-known choices.

Innovative Twists: Introduce progressive twists to acquainted dishes. This can be thru specific flavor combos, possibility additives, or progressive presentation. Innovation sparks curiosity and encourages repeat visits.

4. Consider Dietary Trends

Accommodate Dietary Preferences: Address numerous nutritional alternatives through providing options for vegetarians, vegans, gluten-loose diets, and different famous fitness-aware picks. This inclusivity broadens your client base.

Healthy Alternatives: Incorporate extra healthy alternatives into your menu, in conjunction with grilled options, salads, or dishes with lighter materials. There is a growing preference for wholesome, properly-balanced meals..

5. Seasonal Menu Rotations

Highlight Seasonal Ingredients: Plan seasonal menu rotations to take advantage of glowing, in-season components. Highlighting seasonal produce provides variety to your menu and showcases a self-control to extraordinary.

Limited-Time Specials: Introduce constrained-time specials tied to unique seasons or sports. These exclusives generate exhilaration, create a sense of urgency, and encourage clients to attempt some thing new.

6. Efficient Menu Design

Streamlined Choices: Avoid overwhelming clients with an extensive menu. Streamline alternatives to ensure brief desire-making, reduce wait instances, and hold operational overall performance.

Clear Descriptions: Provide clear and appealing descriptions for each menu object. Highlight unique substances, education techniques, and taste profiles to capture client interest.

7. Pricing Strategy

Competitive Pricing: Establish competitive and transparent pricing. Consider the perceived price of your offerings and ensure that your expenses align with consumer expectations within the nearby marketplace.

Value-Added Combos: Create rate-introduced mixtures or meal gives. Bundling gadgets at a slightly discounted price encourages customers to discover one-of-a-type menu alternatives and complements regular delight.

8. Tech Integration for Ordering

Mobile Ordering: Implement mobile ordering and rate systems. Embracing era improves client comfort, reduces wait times, and enhances not unusual performance on your meals truck operations.

Digital Menu Displays: Explore the usage of digital menu displays. Dynamic shows allow for clean updates, sell constrained-time specials, and contribute to a cutting-edge and attractive patron experience.

9. Feedback Loop and Adaptability

Customer Feedback: Create a remarks loop with the useful resource of encouraging clients to percent their thoughts in your menu. Use online evaluations, social media comments, and direct interactions to understand what works and wherein enhancements may be made.

Adaptability to Trends: Stay abreast of culinary dispositions, every community and global. Be ready to evolve your menu to reflect changing tastes, growing components, and modern-day cooking techniques.

10. Collaborations and Pop-Ups

Collaborative Events: Collaborate with extraordinary food vans or nearby companies for precise activities. Joint efforts introduce variety and may appeal to a shared target market, increasing your reach.

Pop-Up Experiences: Consider internet website hosting pop-up activities to test new menu objects or thoughts. These occasions provide a platform for experimentation and gauge purchaser reaction in advance than making everlasting menu additions.

eleven. Sustainability Practices

Eco-Friendly Menu Options: Integrate sustainability into your menu by manner of using presenting inexperienced packaging, domestically sourced factors, or plant-based options. Demonstrating a determination to sustainability aligns with modern-day purchaser values.

Educate Through the Menu: Use your menu as a platform to educate customers about your sustainability practices. Transparency creates a outstanding brand photo and resonates with environmentally conscious consumers.

12. Consistency in Quality

Quality Control: Maintain consistency within the high-quality of your menu gadgets. Quality control guarantees that clients collect the identical diploma of pride with each go to, building trust and loyalty.

Regular Menu Audits: Conduct everyday menu audits to evaluate the popularity and profitability of each object. Use records to refine the menu, retire underperforming dishes, and introduce new offerings.

Branding and Unique Selling Proposition (USP)

Branding

The workout of giving correct, provider, or commercial enterprise agency a amazing, identifiable identity is known as branding. It includes the improvement of a specific call, logo, design, and normal photograph that devices the entity other than its competition. Effective branding goes beyond seen elements; it encompasses the values, undertaking, and personality of the emblem, growing a ordinary and fantastic experience for customers.

Key Elements of Branding

1. Logo and Visual Identity: A nicely-designed brand is a visual example of the emblem. It want to be specific, effortlessly recognizable, and reflective of the logo's individual.

2. Name: The name of the brand must be memorable, easy to pronounce, and aligned with the emblem's values and identification.

3. Tagline: A concise and impactful tagline can encapsulate the essence of the emblem, talking its middle message to clients.

four. Color Palette and Design: Consistent use of colours, fonts, and layout elements creates a cohesive and visually attractive brand identification.

5. Values and Mission: Clearly defined values and a mission assertion bring the purpose and requirements that manual the emblem's moves.

6. Brand Personality: Brands are regularly personified with exceptional personalities. Whether it's far friendly, present day, or ultra-modern, the brand man or woman influences how customers understand the employer.

7. Customer Experience: The commonplace revel in clients have with the logo, along side interactions with employees, the excellent of products or services, and the logo's presence in the community, contributes to its conventional image.

eight. Consistency: Consistency in branding at some stage in all channels and touchpoints reinforces the emblem's identity and builds believe with customers.

Unique Selling Proposition (USP)

The Unique Selling Proposition (USP) is a distinct element or set of factors that devices a product, service, or enterprise apart from its competitors. It answers the query: "Why ought to customers pick out out your providing over others?" The USP is a completely unique benefit or feature that conveys fee to customers and serves as a key element of the logo's advertising and messaging.

Key Elements of Unique Selling Proposition (USP) encompass the subsequent:

1. Distinctive Features: Identify skills or traits of your supplying that stand out in assessment to competition. This should encompass a very specific issue, a proprietary generation, or a specific company.

2. Value Proposition: Clearly articulate the fee your services or products gives to clients. This goes beyond abilities to cope with the advantages and solutions your imparting delivers.

3. Customer Needs: Understand the goals and goals of your target market. Tailor your USP

to deal with those specific purchaser ache factors or aspirations.

four. Competitive Advantage: Analyze the competitive panorama to pick out what makes your offering advanced or super. Your USP ought to spotlight your aggressive gain.

5. Clarity and Simplicity: Your USP should be easy to recognize and talk. Avoid complexity and strive for clarity in conveying why your supplying is the tremendous choice.

6. Memorability: A memorable USP sticks inside the minds of clients. Craft a message this is memorable, whether or not thru a catchy slogan, a totally precise promise, or a one-of-a-kind characteristic.

7. Consistency Across Marketing: Integrate your USP constantly at some point of marketing substances, advertising and advertising and marketing, and purchaser communications. Reinforce the perfect gain to create a long-lasting affect.

8. Customer Testimonials: Use patron testimonials and achievement memories to validate your USP. Real-life opinions from satisfied clients can upload credibility and authenticity for your particular selling proposition.

In essence, branding and the Unique Selling Proposition artwork hand in hand. Branding establishes the overall identity and character of a organisation, at the same time as the USP focuses on a selected element that gadgets it aside within the market. Together, they shape a compelling narrative that attracts and keeps clients through definitely speaking the unique value and qualities of the brand.

Building a Distinctive Identity (Branding and Unique Selling Proposition (USP) for Your Food Truck Business

Having stated what branding and particular Selling Proposition entail, permit's now take into account a way to construct a very specific identity for a food truck business.

In the competitive landscape of the meals truck enterprise, setting up a sturdy logo identity and a unique promoting proposition (USP) is essential for attracting and maintaining clients.

To craft a compelling logo and USP on your food truck organisation, the following are a few steps to take:

1. Define Your Brand Identity

Mission and Values: Clearly articulate the undertaking and values of your meals truck. Define the ideas that guide your agency, whether or not or now not it's a commitment to great, sustainability, community engagement, or culinary innovation.

Culinary Identity: Communicate your culinary identity and the kinds of flavors or cuisines that set your meals truck aside. Whether it's comfort meals with a twist, global fusion, or a focus on close by materials, make it a crucial a part of your brand tale.

Visual Elements: Develop visually appealing branding factors, alongside aspect a memorable logo, color scheme, and layout factors. Consistency in seen branding within the course of your truck, menu, and promotional substances creates a cohesive and recognizable identity.

2. Craft Your Unique Selling Proposition (USP)

Identify What Sets You Apart: Analyze the strengths and precise abilities of your food truck. This may be a signature dish, a very unique cooking approach, particular components, or a selected culinary concept.

Solve a Problem or Fulfill a Need: Consider how your food truck addresses a particular problem or fulfills a want within the market. Your USP need to awareness at the rate proposition that makes your services stand out.

Emphasize Benefits to Customers: Clearly communicate the blessings clients get hold of by way of manner of choosing your food truck. Whether it's far fantastic taste, short provider, a memorable revel in, or a specific nutritional attention, emphasize the ones benefits.

three. Tailor Your Branding to Your Target Audience

Understand Your Audience: Define your target marketplace and apprehend their alternatives, way of life, and values. Tailor your branding to resonate with this target market, making sure that it appeals to their tastes and aligns with their expectations.

Create Personas: Develop customer personas that constitute your perfect target market segments. Craft your emblem messaging and visuals with those personas in thoughts to create a extra custom designed and attractive experience.

4. Engage in Storytelling

Brand Story: Tell a compelling logo tale that connects with clients emotionally. Share the adventure of your food truck, the foundation behind your dishes, or the precise memories that induced your culinary approach.

Highlight Your Passion: Express your passion for food and the culinary arts. Authenticity in storytelling builds accept as true with and resonates with customers who apprehend the self-control and creativity inside the decrease again of the food.

five. Build a Strong Online Presence

Social Media Engagement: Leverage social media structures to construct a sturdy on-line presence. Share visually attractive content cloth, in the back of-the-scenes glimpses, and purchaser testimonials to create a network spherical your emblem.

Interactive Content: Encourage purchaser engagement through interactive content material. Polls, annoying conditions, and individual-generated content material cloth can foster a enjoy of participation and network amongst your lovers.

6. Create Memorable Experiences

Customer Interactions: Prioritize tremendous customer interactions. Train your staff to offer top notch customer service, developing a memorable experience that extends beyond the taste of the meals.

Event Participation: Participate in community activities, festivals, and community gatherings. Your presence at the ones activities now not exquisite expands your acquire however additionally contributes to the general experience clients companion in conjunction with your emblem.

7. Incorporate Sustainability

Green Practices: If applicable, incorporate sustainability into your emblem messaging. Highlight green practices, along with the usage of biodegradable packaging or sourcing community and herbal components.

Community Involvement: Take detail in collaboration and community activities. Demonstrating a willpower to the local people contributes to a extraordinary logo photo and may foster purchaser loyalty.

8. Adaptability and Consistency

Adapt to Trends: Stay adaptable to emerging meals and customer tendencies. Adjust your menu or services to align with evolving options at the identical time as retaining the middle elements of your brand.

Consistency Across Touchpoints: Ensure consistency in branding at some stage in all touch-factors, which incorporates the meals truck format, menu layout, online presence, and promotional substances. Maintaining consistency strengthens your logo identity and foster agree with.

9. Leverage Customer Testimonials

Customer Reviews and Testimonials: Highlight encouraging comments and opinions from customers. Whether on-line or through in-character interactions, super remarks serves as social proof and reinforces the enchantment of your brand.

Customer Stories: Share customer recollections and research to your on-line systems. Personal anecdotes create a connection among your brand and capability clients, making your food truck greater relatable.

10. Continuous Innovation

Menu Evolution: Demonstrate a dedication to non-prevent innovation. Regularly introduce new menu gadgets, limited-time specials, or seasonal offerings to preserve customers enthusiastic about returning for your food truck.

Adapt to Customer Feedback: Actively seeking out and reply to patron remarks. Use this feedback to refine your services, deal with any issues, and showcase your responsiveness to patron options.

Crafting a strong emblem identification and a completely precise selling proposition is an ongoing system that evolves with your business organisation. By authentically expressing your culinary ardour, addressing patron dreams, and developing memorable critiques, your food truck can set up a completely unique and lasting presence in the hearts and minds of your goal market.

Adapting to Local Tastes and Trends

Adapting to community tastes and inclinations in a meals truck organisation is vital for success. It includes know-how the culinary options, cultural nuances, and rising inclinations of the local community. Follow this step-with the aid of way of-step guide to efficaciously adapt your food truck to community tastes:

1. Conduct Local Market Research

Demographic Analysis: Understand the demographics of the local community. Consider factors together with age, cultural historical past, and profits stages, as those will have an impact on food alternatives.

Visit Local Establishments: Explore nearby eating locations, meals markets, and famous eateries. Observing what is already a fulfillment can offer insights into the flavors and cuisines that attraction to the network.

Gather Customer Feedback: Engage with capability customers thru surveys, tastings, or social media. Ask about their desired community dishes, preferred flavors, and any specific nutritional necessities.

2. Build Relationships with Local Suppliers

Source Local Ingredients: Partner with neighborhood farmers, producers, and carriers. Sourcing sparkling, community additives no longer only helps the community however moreover presents authenticity on your dishes.

Stay Informed about Seasonal Produce: Be aware about the seasonal availability of neighborhood produce. Adjust your menu to include seasonal elements, showcasing the freshness and sort of the region.

Chapter 3: Legalities And Regulations

Licensing and Permits

Starting a meals truck commercial enterprise business enterprise calls for greater than simplest a passion for cooking; it needs an intensive facts of the criminal landscape, particularly on the subject of licensing and permits. Complying with regulatory necessities guarantees your meals truck operates resultseasily, avoids criminal problems, and protects both your commercial enterprise and your clients.

Here's an in depth manual on licensing and lets in for your meals truck:

1. Business Structure and Registration

Choose a Business Structure: Decide on a suitable business employer shape, together with sole proprietorship, LLC, or industrial organisation organisation. Your desire will affect the form of licenses and lets in you need.

Register Your Business: Register your food truck commercial corporation with the brilliant government. This often entails filing workplace work with the close by or country authorities and acquiring a very specific agency identification extensive variety.

2. Health Department Permits

Food Handler's Permit: Ensure that you and your personnel acquire the critical food handler's allows. This is often a requirement to illustrate a number one expertise of meals safety practices.

Mobile Food Vendor License: Apply for a cellular food supplier license from the nearby fitness branch. This license demonstrates compliance with fitness and safety requirements specific to cell food organizations.

Regular Health Inspections: Prepare for and go through everyday health inspections. These inspections may rise up randomly or on a scheduled foundation, ensuring that your meals truck maintains cleanliness and adheres to food protection policies.

three. Vehicle Licenses and Inspections

Vehicle Registration: Ensure that your meals truck is registered with the outstanding transportation government. This entails acquiring a car registration code and complying with any hints associated with industrial vehicles.

Department of Motor Vehicles (DMV): Check with the close by DMV for any extra requirements associated with company motors. This also can consist of safety inspections and adherence to precise vehicle necessities.

four. Location and Zoning Permits

Research Zoning Regulations: Understand neighborhood zoning regulations that observe to cell meals carriers. Zoning lets in may also additionally dictate wherein you may perform your food truck, which incorporates restrictions on proximity to residential areas and one-of-a-kind businesses.

Apply for Zoning Permits: Submit packages for zoning allows to the nearby making plans or zoning branch. Ensure that your proposed places align with the zoning felony tips in region.

5. Fire Department Permits

Fire Safety Inspection: Schedule a fire safety inspection in your meals truck. This is vital for making sure that your car complies with fireside safety requirements, collectively with the proper installation of fireside extinguishers and exclusive protection machine.

Fire Department Permits: Obtain any critical lets in from the fireside branch. This might also additionally include permits associated with the usage of propane or one of a type cooking fuels on your meals truck.

6. Environmental Permits

Waste Disposal Permits: Check in case you need lets in for waste disposal. Proper disposal of meals waste, grease, and terrific materials is essential, and permits can be required to illustrate compliance with environmental guidelines.

Sustainability Considerations: If you're incorporating sustainable practices, including composting or the usage of inexperienced packaging, make sure that you observe any applicable environmental regulations and attain the crucial lets in.

7. Alcohol Beverage Control (ABC) License

Considerations for Alcohol Sales: If your meals truck plans to sell alcoholic beverages, you can need an Alcohol Beverage Control (ABC) license. Be aware of the proper hints concerning alcohol income at cell food institutions.

Apply for an ABC License: Submit an utility for an ABC license to the relevant state or community authorities. The machine can also additionally moreover include ancient beyond assessments and compliance with precise guidelines for accountable alcohol provider.

8. Special Event Permits

Participating in Events: If your food truck plans to take part in unique occasions, gala's, or markets, test if particular event allows are required. Event organizers also can have specific requirements for taking factor carriers.

Temporary Food Establishment Permits: Obtain quick food reputation quo allows if your food truck might be operating at sports for a constrained duration. These licences regularly embody the requirements and situations.

nine. Tax Identification Numbers and Sales Tax Permits

Apply for a Tax ID Number: Obtain a Tax Identification Number (TIN) or Employer Identification Number (EIN) from the IRS. This extensive variety is crucial for tax reporting purposes and may be required at the same time as the use of for extraordinary licenses.

Sales Tax Permits: Check along with your u . S .'s tax branch to decide if you want a profits tax permit. If your food truck sells taxable devices, along with organized food, you'll likely want to build up and remit earnings tax.

10. Insurance Requirements

Commercial Vehicle Insurance: Ensure your meals truck has authentic sufficient business enterprise vehicle insurance. This insurance is vital for shielding your enterprise and complying with jail necessities for commercial enterprise cars.

Liability Insurance: Obtain legal responsibility coverage to shield your organisation from potential claims related to injuries, foodborne illnesses, or unique incidents which could stand up for your meals truck.

11. Renewals and Compliance

Stay Informed about Renewals: Keep track of renewal dates for all licenses and lets in. Renewals are often required every 12 months, and failure to renew on time can cause fines or the suspension of your business employer operations.

Stay Compliant with Regulations: Regularly have a look at community, kingdom, and federal policies to ensure ongoing compliance. Regulations may additionally additionally moreover exchange, and staying knowledgeable helps you adapt your business corporation practices for this reason.

Navigating the area of licensing and allows for a meals truck enterprise organization requires diligence, employer, and a proactive approach. By information and adhering to the prison necessities noted through way of manner of fitness departments, zoning government, and different regulatory our bodies, you may establish a sturdy basis for the success and sturdiness of your meals truck project.

Health and Safety Standards

Maintaining excessive health and safety requirements is paramount in the meals enterprise, and on the subject of a cellular meals truck enterprise, it becomes even extra critical. Ensuring the protection of your clients and the integrity of your food is not simplest a crook requirement however moreover fundamental for building agree with and a splendid popularity.

Outlined beneath are some steps for upholding fitness and protection requirements on your meals truck commercial company:

1. Compliance with Health Department Regulations

Obtain Necessary Permits: Secure all required fitness allows from the nearby fitness department earlier than taking walks your meals truck. This often consists of a Mobile Food Vendor License, indicating that your business enterprise complies with fitness and protection guidelines.

Undergo Health Inspections: Regularly go through health inspections as mandated by way of manner of way of neighborhood health authorities. These inspections make sure that your food truck meets cleanliness, sanitation, and meals coping with standards.

2. Food Handler Training

Certify Staff: Ensure that each one body of humans people dealing with food are licensed meals handlers. Many jurisdictions require food handler training, which covers topics which includes proper hygiene, stable meals managing practices, and preventing cross-contamination.

Provide Ongoing Training: Conduct regular schooling periods to keep your personnel up to date at the present day-day fitness and safety protocols. This is specifically vital at the same time as introducing new menu devices or imposing adjustments in meals coaching techniques.

three. Safe Food Handling Practices

Temperature Control: Adhere to strict temperature manipulate requirements for every hot and bloodless food devices. Monitor and record temperatures regularly to prevent bacterial increase and make sure food protection.

Avoid Cross-Contamination: Implement approaches to prevent skip-contamination amongst uncooked and cooked elements. Use separate decreasing forums, utensils, and storage regions for uncooked and equipped-to-eat elements.

Proper Thawing and Cooking: Follow proper approaches for thawing frozen materials and cooking them to the recommended inner temperatures. This allows get rid of risky bacteria and guarantees the safety of the food you serve.

Hygienic Food Preparation: Emphasize personal hygiene amongst your frame of personnel. This consists of using clean uniforms, frequent handwashing, and the usage of gloves whilst managing ready-to-devour food devices.

4. Sanitation Practices

Daily Cleaning Routine: Establish a complete each day cleansing ordinary on your food truck. Regularly smooth and sanitize all surfaces, utensils, and gadget to prevent the buildup of contaminants.

Effective Dishwashing: Ensure that your food truck has a right dishwashing station. Use powerful sanitizers and detergents to easy dishes, utensils, and cooking machine.

Regular Deep Cleaning: Schedule ordinary deep cleaning commands for difficult-to-attain areas and device. This consists of cleaning air float structures, refrigeration gadgets, and one-of-a-kind additives that may accumulate dirt and debris.

five. Allergen Management

Transparent Menu Labeling: Clearly label all menu devices with ability allergens. This transparency permits customers with meals hypersensitive reactions make informed choices and decreases the hazard of accidental exposure.

Separate Cooking Areas: If viable, designate separate cooking regions or machine for allergen-loose menu gadgets. This minimizes the risk of flow-touch and guarantees the safety of customers with food allergies.

6. Safe Water Supply

Regular Water Quality Checks: Ensure the exquisite of the water utilized in meals steerage. Regularly take a look at the water supply for contaminants, and address any problems right away to prevent waterborne illnesses.

Sanitary Water Storage: If your meals truck has a water storage tank, make certain that it is regularly wiped clean and clean upd. Proper water storage prevents bacterial increase and contamination.

7. Waste Management

Secure Waste Disposal: Implement secure waste disposal practices. Dispose of meals waste and unique substances in a manner that forestalls infection and minimizes the risk of attracting pests.

Separate Waste Bins: Use separate packing containers for unique forms of waste, which includes recyclables and natural waste. Clearly label and show waste disposal to ensure proper sorting.

8. Emergency Preparedness

First Aid Kit: Maintain a properly-stocked first beneficial resource package to your meals truck. Ensure that all body of human beings individuals understand the region of the package and are educated in fundamental first useful aid techniques.

Emergency Response Plan: Develop an emergency response plan that includes approaches for coping with foodborne ailments, accidents, or precise emergencies. Train your staff at the protocol to comply with in case of an emergency.

nine. Regular Equipment Maintenance

Schedule Equipment Checks: Regularly investigate and maintain all device. Malfunctioning device can pose safety risks and compromise the pleasant of your meals.

Calibrate Thermometers: Calibrate thermometers regularly to ensure correct temperature readings. Reliable temperature monitoring is important for stopping foodborne ailments.

10. Communication and Transparency

Customer Allergen Inquiries: Train your frame of people to address customer inquiries about allergens. Provide accurate data about the elements used on your dishes to address clients with dietary regulations.

Display Health Inspection Certificates: Display your health inspection certificate prominently to your food truck. This demonstrates transparency and reassures customers that your business meets fitness and safety standards.

eleven. Continuous Improvement

Encourage Feedback: Encourage customers and workforce to offer feedback on fitness and safety practices. Use this feedback to pick out out regions for improvement and enforce essential adjustments.

Regular Audits and Assessments: Conduct everyday internal audits of your health and protection practices. Periodically determine your techniques and make adjustments primarily based on evolving requirements or instructions found out.

By prioritizing fitness and protection necessities to your meals truck agency, you not best take a look at tips but furthermore create a basis for fulfillment. Building a way of lifestyles of protection interior your crew and continuously implementing high-quality practices will not high-quality guard your clients but moreover contribute to the prolonged-time period success and excessive quality popularity of your food truck venture.

Compliance with Local Regulations

Following the under steps will help you navigate and ensure compliance with nearby tips:

1. Research Local Zoning Regulations

Understand Zoning Laws: Begin by means of the usage of mastering close by zoning prison hints to decide in which your food truck is allowed to perform. Different areas can also have guidelines on cell meals providers, which incorporates distance requirements from faculties or barriers on specific zones.

Contact the Zoning Department: Reach out to the community zoning department to make clean any questions you have got approximately permissible locations for your food truck. They can offer information on specific zones in which mobile food vending is permitted.

Obtain Necessary Zoning Permits: Apply for and accumulate any required zoning allows earlier than jogging your food truck. Failure to comply with zoning suggestions may additionally additionally result in fines or crook repercussions.

2. Health Department Compliance

Secure Health Permits: Obtain all vital health allows from the nearby health department earlier than starting your food truck agency. This regularly includes a Mobile Food Vendor License and permits for food guidance and managing.

Schedule Regular Health Inspections: Schedule and go through normal health inspections to make sure your food truck keeps compliance with sanitation and safety necessities. Any problem located all through inspections need to be constant proper away.

Follow Food Safety Protocols: Implement and positioned into impact strict food safety protocols, together with right temperature manipulate, prevention of pass-contamination, and hygienic food coping with practices.

3. Licensing and Business Registration

Choose a Business Structure: Select a appropriate organization shape, collectively with sole proprietorship, LLC, or company. The decided on shape affects licensing necessities and criminal duties.

Register Your Business: Register your meals truck enterprise with the best close by government. This often entails filing vital office paintings, acquiring a enterprise license, and securing a very unique organisation identity amount.

Renew Licenses Annually: Ensure that each one business enterprise licenses and allows are renewed every year. Keep song of renewal dates to keep away from working with expired licenses, that could result in fines or commercial employer closure.

4. Vehicle Licensing and Inspection

Vehicle Registration: Ensure that your food truck is properly registered with the Department of Motor Vehicles (DMV). Commercial automobile registration can be required for agency-operated cars.

Routine Vehicle Inspections: Schedule normal inspections on your food truck to make sure it meets protection requirements. Regular maintenance and adherence to car guidelines make a contribution to steady and compliant operations.

5. Fire Safety Compliance

Fire Extinguisher Installation: Install fireside extinguishers in precise regions of your meals truck as required through community fireplace safety guidelines. Regularly take a look at and preserve extinguishers to make certain they may be in strolling situation.

Training on Fire Safety Measures: Train your frame of employees on fireside protection measures, along with emergency evacuation techniques and the proper use of hearth extinguishers. A properly-organized organization is important for managing surprising incidents.

6. Environmental Regulations

Waste Disposal Compliance: Adhere to close by guidelines concerning waste disposal. Implement right waste management practices, which incorporates recycling and disposal of meals waste in compliance with environmental requirements.

Sustainability Practices: If your food truck includes sustainability practices, collectively with the use of green packaging, make certain that the ones practices align with network environmental policies.

7. Alcohol Beverage Control (ABC) Compliance

Understand Alcohol Sales Regulations: If your food truck plans to promote alcoholic drinks, make your self acquainted with nearby Alcohol Beverage Control (ABC) recommendations. This consists of obtaining the critical licenses and adhering to responsible issuer recommendations.

Apply for ABC Licenses: Submit programs for any required ABC licenses. This gadget also can contain records exams and verification of compliance with particular regulations for alcohol income.

Chapter 4: A Look Back At Food Truck History

Food automobiles have grow to be more and more famous since the 2008 monetary disaster, and they'll be now seen as a legitimate form of eating place on par with circle of relatives-style or fast food. A growing style of could-be restaurateurs are interested in launching meals truck groups because to their low startup charges and growing reputation as tremendous venues for starting a career within the food enterprise. These days, food trucks provide nearly something you may don't forget, along with grilled cheese sandwiches, cupcakes, and taco-waffle hybrids. Beyond the identical old street meals fare, food vans are more and more offering latest, locally produced, artisan menu alternatives.

The Growth of Food Trucks

Food changed into offered on the streets inside the past due 17th century, whilst housing conditions have been cramped, and loads of human beings lacked the method to cook dinner dinner dinner their very very own meals. Food carriers have lengthy been a common sight in towns internationally, promoting their wares from makeshift carts or street kitchens.

Roy Choi have come to be one of the most critical leaders within the enterprise very quickly after launching Kogi in Los Angeles in 2008. Serving Korean BBQ, it's miles identified as one of the first gourmet food automobiles in the United States.

By 2021, there will be over 24,000 food cars running inside the US, bringing in an entire of $1 billion in income every year, predicts research employer IBISWorld. In the period in-between, boom was expected to attain 7.Five% amongst 2015 and 2020. 1 Because nation and network recommendations vary from america of the united states to nation, meals vehicles might be more everyday in a few areas than others.

Typical Websites

Food automobiles have historically been associated with short and easy food like warm puppies or ethnic avenue food that may be observed in busy city regions. As their menus have superior and their recognition has grown, food trucks are in reality more often visible in places aside from simply busy street corners in densely populated towns.

At festivals, gala's, stay performance events, wearing activities, and awesome public gatherings, meals trucks are a regular sight. They paintings in suburban regions and smaller cities. Food trucks now provide attendees a greater variety of alternatives, plenty of which might be greater healthy than easy concession stands at huge sports.

Some food vehicles are operated as satellite tv for pc locations of installation ingesting locations, while others began as lots much less expensive alternatives to standard consuming locations. Occasionally, famous eateries growth to contain a food truck as a manner to serve their scrumptious meals to customers throughout huge gatherings or on unique unique events. It also may be performed as a brand-promotional marketing approach. For instance, a few customers may also moreover find a restaurant via using ordering from a food truck all through a get-collectively out of doors.

Rules Regarding Food Trucks

Like any small commercial corporation, running a food truck consists of adhering to recommendations and acquiring the essential licenses. You can even need to draft an in depth advertising approach. There is a restricted supply of meals truck permits in cities like New York, Los Angeles, and Chicago. The places and hours that food cars can park are likewise governed thru legal recommendations in towns and cities. If you're deliberating launching a meals truck commercial organisation, get greater facts thru the use of speaking with the network zoning authority.

Some towns set guidelines at the locations and hours that food cars can feature, based on the quantity of brick-and-mortar consuming locations which can be open for business enterprise corporation. A smaller metropolis with numerous famous consuming locations in its downtown might also moreover limit the type of blocks that meals vehicles are allowed to function internal in the course of particular hours to keep away from overwhelming the region with meals alternatives.

Crucial Information for People Launching a Food Truck Company

Starting a food truck agency at the bypass is a great way to increase into the food company or increase sales at eateries that already perform. Although meals motors have historically furnished sandwiches, hot puppies, and ice cream, the sector has considering the fact that grown to provide a substantial kind of gourmand components. Nowadays, meals trucks that serve consuming places provide a big form of dishes, collectively with Kung Pao fowl, gourmet cupcakes, and smokey BBQ ribs.

However, beginning a food truck isn't an clean feat. Before starting a food truck business business enterprise, you have to be privy to the subsequent 10 topics:

1. Not every city allow food vans. Initiating a meals truck enterprise starts with figuring out whether or not parking is authorized wherein you want to park. Choosing a place for your corporation and the laws which can be both now in impact or are expected to be exceeded quick have to be your priority. There are obstacles for mobile traders in tremendous municipalities and localities.

2. Food trucks rate some of coins. Even with its sizable price financial savings over a regular restaurant, a meals truck will though price you hundreds of dollars. Even used ones can run you over $15,000, or even then, they'll want to be customized to fit your specific wishes. You might require coins from

a financial organization, the Small Business Administration, or buyers if you do not have loads of coins available. It's moreover vital to pay ongoing fees like fuel, car protection, parking, and network license fees, to call some, further to the direct expenses of marketing and getting equipped food.

Before doing it, make certain to do some look at.

3. The fee of startup exceeds the acquisition price of the truck. Even in case you buy a brand new vehicle, which may cost a little as an awful lot as $one hundred and fifty,000 or extra, you'll but need to keep the truck's appearance with paint, lights, and signs and symptoms and symptoms. Then there are the charges of food buying, hiring a professional kitchen, renting a generator or propane, and getting insurance (both for the commercial corporation and your automobile). After that, you may periodically want to replace the tires, oil, and wiper fluid.

four. A food truck that is commonly at the pass requires the essential licenses and allows. It may be critical if you want to exercise for unique licenses and lets in primarily based mostly on in that you intend to conduct business organisation. If there can be a restriction on the amount of lets in that can be issued in a excellent region, meals truck groups might probable ought to wait a completely prolonged period. Permits can rate taken into consideration one among a type amounts and frequently want to be renewed each yr. In addition to running licenses, you can need to reap parking allows to obtain pinnacle lessen down-aspect real property.

5. A food truck's operation needs cautious attention of fitness and safety. If your business enterprise gives food provider to the general public, take the important precautions to make sure the safety of each employees and clients. Food need to be treated, cooked, and served on the right temperature in hygienic situations. Obtaining

a health license is a prerequisite to starting up a enterprise enterprise. Your community health inspector will walk you thru the recommendations essential to guarantee the protection of your meals truck enterprise.

6. Restaurants and meals automobiles don't continually combination. It's possible that nearby food truck parking will now not be appreciated via close by eateries due to the fierce opposition inside the grocery store. If your commercial enterprise genuinely serves dessert, do not forget setting up keep subsequent to a burger and heat dog region.

7. The region of a food truck enterprise determines its success. One of a food truck's primary advantages over a normal eating facility is its capability to deliver food to clients. But you have to realise wherein your customers are. Everything is based upon on in that you park and what number of human beings are walking around in a crowded community. It won't be certainly well well worth the money to fight for a niche within

the direction of the walking lunch hour in sure busy regions.

8. Food vehicles are still a viable region to consume. From the menu alternatives to the exceptional of the business enterprise, purchasers want to get the impact that they have got been to a restaurant. To get move returned clients, think about your meals truck as a mobile eating place. The excellent possible superb, company, and reduce attraction are provided.

9. Social networking can be quite useful for food cars. Mobile food truck groups commonly use social media net websites like Facebook, Twitter, and Instagram to sell their manufacturers. You can tweet updates on profits and different promotions in addition in your each day schedule.

10. A meals truck calls for some of art work to carry out. Operating a small enterprise calls for a number of paintings. It way installing masses of extra time and wearing numerous hats. On any given day, you can be the put

together dinner dinner, waiter, dishwasher, bookkeeper, and accountant. It is genuinely fulfilling, but it isn't always constantly a glamorous assignment. Before deciding on to come to be a food truck proprietor, have a look at the requirements and behavior a reality check.

The food truck is one of the most famous restaurants standards nowadays. Even a Food Network software, The Great Food Truck Race, is dedicated to it. Compared to standard brick-and-mortar ingesting places, they offer low startup charges and minimum overhead. However, a food truck remains a commercial enterprise business enterprise, and prefer every other, it calls for paintings and resolution to achieve success.

How to Start a Food Truck Business

There can be massive money inside the meals truck industrial employer. If you've got ever belief of scrumptious cooking food instant, this educational on starting a meals truck enterprise is for you.

Foodies with an entrepreneurial spirit may be capable of release a meals truck corporation in lieu of a conventional brick-and-mortar eating place, even though they lack the capital.

A meals truck is a large automobile organized with a kitchen for cooking and serving food. They have come to be increasingly properly-favored and are taking the country via using storm. Considering how steeply-priced it is to open a restaurant, loads of marketers determine to run meals vehicles as an alternative.

Before proceeding, make certain you've got all of the statistics you need, collectively with the start charges, investment options, places of meals automobiles, and extra.

Initial charges related to food trucks.

A food truck corporation's preliminary startup prices are contingent upon numerous factors. There are furthermore one-time and area-particular costs.

One-time beginning charges embody shopping for a meals truck, installing a component-of-sale (POS) gadget, wrapping a truck, designing a internet site, shopping for place of business components, advertising, and PR, in addition to any consulting, prison, or professional expenses. Although now not all-inclusive, this listing gives aspiring food truck proprietors an idea of a number of the startup charges.

"We paid in fact $15,000 for the meals truck itself, however we didn't apprehend that we'd spent more than double that to have it modified to wholesome the nearby hearth and fitness suggestions, which variety quite considerably relying on the municipality," says Rachel Angulo, the proprietor of the La Cocinita food truck.

Then there are the ordinary fees, which embody credit score card processing, device apartment, gasoline, payroll, and permissions and licenses that want to be obtained for every new food truck organisation; those range relying on the location.

The initial funding needed to begin a meals truck business enterprise can variety from $28,000 to $114,000, depending to your precise situation.

According to Food Truck Empire, you must fee range for the following extra in advance fees at the same time as launching a meals truck employer:

Insurance fees variety from $2,000 to $four,000 regular with three hundred and sixty five days, and the first product stock is among $1,000 and $2,000 in value.

Payment processing: $200 to $1,000

Commissariat expenses: $4 hundred to $1,200

Permits and licenses: $100 to $500

Important commands located: Starting a food truck business enterprise can variety in rate from $28,000 to $114,000, regardless of the truth that this isn't typically the case.

Ways to resource food motors via sponsorship.

Obtaining investment will in all likelihood be the most essential project you face on the identical time as beginning a meals truck business corporation.

Your first goal have to be a properly-written business employer plan. You want to additionally have top notch non-public and business organisation credit score rating rating to increase your possibilities of being widely wide-spread for a commercial enterprise mortgage.

There are precise, more current tactics to raise capital in your new food truck industrial agency.

The following are a few low-price businesses start techniques:

Speak with an character who presently operates a meals truck approximately a lease or rental agreement.

Start with an low cost, used cart or trailer.

Start merchandising at farmer's markets, pop-up stores, or sincere cubicles.

Look for sponsors in case your truck concept includes offering a network carrier or advantage.

Have a communique with rich eating place proprietors regarding taking walks a food truck for his or her organization.

You may also additionally furthermore qualify for a loan enhance in case you presently use a charge processor.

Write a meals truck advertising technique.

A well-written and cutting-edge-day commercial enterprise organization approach is important for any food truck proprietor to have, and it have to be the first thing you do at the same time as identifying to begin a food truck business company. It will help you enchantment to consumers, solid investment, and get off the floor.

According to WebstaurantStore, your industrial organisation method wishes to have the subsequent factors:

1. An authorities precis. An government summary is a synopsis of your marketing strategy that introduces your company. It ought to be brief because of the fact next sections of the plan will deal with the specific information.

2. A synopsis of the agency; on this section, give an cause for your identification and what distinguishes you as a business business enterprise; spotlight the market section you're serving; and offer an explanation for why customers must select you over your competition.

three. Market research. In this segment, you will outline the characteristics, dreams, venues, and methods of your aim marketplace to draw them on your agency. You can also even show that you are aware about the state of the community food market and supply an motive for how your enterprise will impact it.

four. Management and company. Next, outline your corporation's prison industrial employer entity shape (sole proprietorship, LLC, partnership, and so forth.). Include a list of the company's shareholders and their possession stakes. Don't neglect approximately to encompass critical humans, like your control group, on the facet of their credentials, earnings statistics, and earlier positions held.

Chapter 5: How To Locate Food Vehicles

Even though Craigslist remains a high-quality area to begin your are looking for, there are several new assets obtainable, like:

Local online classifieds: These are a amazing opportunity as used vehicles are a great deal less high-priced and, if they may be nearby, can be without problem tested.

Online national classifieds: These can appreciably boom the choice, but due to the fact you won't probable be capable of view the truck earlier than pickup, make certain to get as tons information as you can from the vendor.

New, high-quality vans: Although the maximum steeply-priced preference, that is the first-rate way to assure that your truck meets all pointers and specs and may be custom designed to fulfill your necessities.

Leasing and franchising: Leasing a truck from a massive national leasing enterprise or a network leasing business enterprise may be an desire for you. Another alternative is to franchise a car from an gift organisation. One drawback to bear in mind is that you may no longer oversee the products, advertising and marketing, or menu.

Here are some locations to look for the first-class food truck:

Wandering Appetite,

Made use of vending, and

Empire Food Truck.

Options for mobile element of sale

Most food truck clients favor to pay with coins, regardless of the tremendous use of credit score playing cards and contact purchases.

According to Angulo, "We've constantly used Square, and we are glad with each their POS carrier and credit score rating card processing."

Ordered from least steeply-priced to most state-of-the-art are the subsequent options for handling earnings.

Sales the usage of honestly cash and the cash discipline.

Advantages: Fairly priced. You can get a locked container for a good buy much less than $20.

Drawbacks: You can not take credit score score card payments, and it does no longer hold track of profits or food inventories.

No ordinary charges

The fee-effectiveness of a cash container and a cellular card reader is obvious. Mobile processors honestly price a fee for every swipe, however gaining access to the processing company requires a Wi-Fi connection and/or a robust information plan.

Cons: Most cellular CPUs have a minimal stock tool and restricted extra talents.

Ongoing prices: Fees associated with processing mobile facts and credit score and debit playing cards

Cash container + POS tool + cellular processing has the following drawbacks: greater monthly provider rate; hardware costs; cellular credit rating and debit card processing; profits and stock monitoring.

Ongoing costs include feasible hardware expenses, monthly POS carrier prices, card processing expenses, and cellular statistics company fees.

The benefits of running a food truck business Business possession: Although going for walks a organisation can be difficult, there are various tax benefits, so as a minimum there can be a few remedy from that detail.

independence: As a food truck entrepreneur, you have had been given a remarkable deal of independence. You might also additionally select out your vendors, employees, events to promote at, and menu gadgets. You moreover have entire manage over your marketing and marketing and advertising, social media, and scheduling.

Mobility: Angulo claims that having the energy to relocate your agency to certainly one of a type places primarily based mostly on name for at one-of-a-type instances of the day, on precise days of the week, and so on., is a big advantage.

The annoying situations that food truck businesses come across.

Hours: Operating a meals truck commercial agency generally involves working lengthy hours. This is because handling a meals truck organization entails duties together with steering, advertising, occasion making plans, cleansing, truck preservation, bookkeeping, tax responsibilities, and shopping.

Market and opposition: To increase your possibilities of success, behavior in-depth market research. Other meals motors will in reality compete with you.

Zoning and ordinances: Depending on the network, there are one in every of a type regulations on wherein and the way long you may park your food truck. Be certain you are knowledgeable of the policies in any location in which you want to conduct commercial enterprise to avoid fines and outcomes.

Rules and licenses for meals trucks

It is imperative which you check out the ability net web sites for your business enterprise and don't forget any applicable licenses and regulations.

Here are some critical subjects to be aware about:

Food protection: You need to look at neighborhood meals protection guidelines similar to a few different eating place inside the location. Contact the nearby health authority to discover extra, in conjunction with despite the fact that you may use your personal centers or in case you have to prepare all your meals in a business kitchen.

Seller's allow: In wonderful states, meals truck proprietors are required to apply for a dealer's permit, which permits them to shop for food and machine at wholesale prices while not having to pay earnings tax.

Zoning and parking: Research ability restrictions on where you can park your truck earlier than starting your corporation. You can get assist from the close by and town motor vehicle departments. These rules might also encompass cut-off dates on parking, zoning prison hints that distinguish among business and noncommercial makes use of, or restrictions at the proximity of your corporation to distinctive groups.

Driver's license: Depending on your nation and the size of your automobile, you could require a commercial corporation reason force's license to legally perform a food truck because your organisation relies upon on a automobile. Each driving strain should possess the critical workplace work and training.

Fire certificates: Each u.S.A. Of the us has remarkable necessities for obtaining a fire certificate, so in case you plan to use the truck's gadget for meals guidance, you may probable want to go through a hearth department inspection.

Employee Identification Number (EIN): An organisation identity amount (EIN), a federal tax identity extensive range issued via the IRS to pick out a business organization organisation, is needed if you plan to lease employees. With an EIN, you could open a employer economic organization account and start setting up your organisation's credit rating records.

Check the hints on your community u . S . Earlier than founding your organization.

Business permits and licenses: Operating a food truck requires an entire lot of licenses, much like any other type of business company. These include a nation income tax permit and a DBA, every of that are low-cost and smooth to advantage.

Section Two

Ideas for Food Trucks

There are hundreds of opportunities for small enterprise owners within the food truck business enterprise. Instead of wanting to put money into a whole brick and mortar business enterprise organization, you can begin your personal food provider agency with handiest a automobile, cooking utensils, and materials. The first step in launching a meals truck commercial enterprise organisation is developing with the right idea. On the opportunity hand, you may possibly start a meals truck franchise. If you may as an alternative take your very own way, you may draw concept from the favored alternatives stated under.

Why Is Owning a Food Truck Justified?

Owners of food vans get masses of blessings over traditional eating place operators. If the urge is powerful in you to release your private employer and you have a few experience on this region, do not forget the following benefits of mobile ingesting locations:

Low preliminary outlay

The capacity to set up at well-known venues and occasions

Parking your truck and riding it across the metropolis will function unfastened industrial.

The ability to complement more earnings streams like catering or a physical region

Easy growth with the resource of purchasing greater automobiles

The Most Creative Ideas for Food Truck Businesses

It's time to get yourself up to speed with the best-of-a-kind food truck organisation thoughts in case you're prepared to assignment into the meals truck region. Here are numerous options for capacity food truck operators.

1. The meals truck serving veganism

Vegan food is a warm difficulty remember in the meals organisation. The meals served in those cell kitchens want to often be plant-based absolutely. Lunch clients in contemporary areas might possibly find them appealing because they're healthy.

2. Food Truck at the Street

Usually, factors from a road meals dealer are supposed to be eaten right away. The most well-known dishes on this class are pierogi, bahn mi, arepas, and sliders.

3. Fast Food Truck

This form of car would probable look like a force-thru in a constrained area where customers can also method it.

four. Van for Ice Cream

Ice cream vehicles are the most conventional preference in the food truck region. Even despite the fact that a number of them camp out, they regularly bypass via residential regions.

5. Fresh Catch is served by using manner of manner of a seafood truck.

These food vehicles are commonly determined in large densities with the aid of the coast. Nearly any seafood choice available in a traditional brick and mortar eating place may be bought there, such as nearby favorites like lobster rolls in the Northeast.

6. Connoisseur food truck serving hamburgers

Their area of expertise is hamburgers which might be cooked glowing. Many of them function unusual factors, like onion jewelry, fried eggs, and jalapenos.

7. Truck for Cattle

Serve conventional meat, cheese, and sour cream dishes. Alternately, use particular food sold from neighborhood carriers.

8. Pancake cart

Serve this meal with toppings which incorporates cream cheese, whipped cream, or sprinkles on a stick or in a paper tray for handy carrying.

nine. Delivery of chicken that has been fried

Serve tenders, legs, or one-of-a-kind portable food with an abundance of sauce alternatives.

10. Dog-Friendly Food Truck

If you are keen on on foot with animals, keep in mind launching a cope with-selling business company in puppy-extraordinary institutions like dog parks.

11. Food Truck on the Agricultural Market

This precise food truck corporation could set up stores and offer clean produce or comparable topics at neighborhood farmers markets.

12. Starbucks in Motion

Coffee vans or stands can promote a significant type of uniqueness drinks or blends. Particular interest have to be paid to organisation districts or places with heavy early foot pastime.

thirteen. Transport Pork

There are numerous clean-to-promote red meat merchandise that may be offered on the road. Think pulled red meat sliders, beef ribs, or some detail wrapped with bacon.

14. Donuts Dunkin'

The terrific time to consume donuts is at some stage in the breakfast hour. Still, you may promote the ones movable products almost anywhere.

15. Burger Place

Hot dogs are a famous snack object at own family-exceptional occasions. Serve traditional dishes or top with particular substances.

16. Open Kitchen

A community kitchen would possibly attention on underprivileged populations or parents which may be improving the neighborhood at the identical time as serving cuisine prepared the use of network merchandise.

17. BBQ Burger Truck

For companies with constrained location, little bins are a available way to promote fish fry dishes like ribs, brisket, and mac and cheese.

18. A food truck serving cheese

If you want your menu to be numerous, undergo in thoughts going with a cheese concern depend. Think of foods like grilled cheese, mac & cheese, and fried cheese sticks.

19. Dessert Van

Cupcakes are a conventional and practical dessert desire. Provide this to folks that are searching for a candy deal with after a meal in places with a number of eating places or different food institutions.

20. Food trailers for the duration of carnivals

At carnivals and comparable activities, concession stands promoting funnel desserts, sno cones, and other such sweets are very famous.

21. Food cart

Serve pizza slices for an smooth and well-known dessert.

22. Sandwich truck

Sandwiches are portable and to be had in a full-size variety. Serve a large variety of cuisines or attention on one.

23. Fusion of Gourmet Food Trucks

Fusion cuisine blends first-rate culinary genres. Think of tacos with orange fowl or pizza with barbeque sauce.

Chapter 6: The Location Of A Food Truck Purchase

Food automobiles abound. Are you attempting to shop for one? A budget is a critical starting point. Following that, determine if you need to shop for, hire, or hire a food truck. Buying one on eBay or Craigslist consists of a few threats. The following is a list of the nice places to shop for food cars.

Best Locations to Buy a Food Truck

You want to realise a manner to start a food truck agency further to buying a car. A organisation method for a food truck need to be created in advance than operations begin. You'll ought to ordinary investment and pick out a market. In awesome additives of the usa, you can require a fitness permit. You then have to choose out the menu items. If greater food carrier tool is needed, upload it.

Buying a food truck is one of the most essential choices. This is a list to help you get going.

Buying a Food Truck thru eBay

The maximum high priced and time-eating a part of the gadget is the preliminary buy of one of these vans. Purchasing this kind of on eBay has benefits and downsides. Repairs and safety may be pricey. When searching out a used truck, look for photos which might be of a high excellent. It is important to remember the tires, seats, outdoor, and inner.

Considering starting a organisation on eBay? These are the blessings.

eBay sellers need to fulfill precise necessities. They require no longer satisfactory a verified PayPal account however also

not unusual assessment of dealer regular overall performance. You can take a look at the seller's profile to ensure they may be a sincere issuer. It is positioned to the proper of each bid.

Buying a food truck from eBay is mostly a constant transaction. The platform

capabilities in tandem with PayPal's protection mechanisms.

There are additional protection precautions. Clicking at the variety adjoining to the vendor's username will choose that provider. You'll be redirected to their comments net web site through it.

There are fine terrible elements for company proprietors wishing to buy on eBay.

Recognize the costs. Reasonably priced food truck fees aren't determined with the resource of a few eBay investors. At other instances, you could find out extra cheap costs. It's an remarkable concept to perform a little studies earlier than committing. You can be able to negotiate a less high priced price through doing this.

Not each eBay seller will answer questions previous to a sale. Verify that their maximum modern-day touch statistics is protected in the Contact Seller phase.

Exercise warning on the equal time as undertaking transactions that display up outside of eBay. No consumer or provider safety applications will study to you in case you skip beforehand with those.

Lastly, don't forget that secondhand automobiles are to begin with less pricey than new ones. But in the end, preservation and protection will rate cash. These can increase a commercial company's charges.

Craigslist food truck vicinity

Craigslist works nicely if you're looking for an easy way to shop for a meals truck. These are a few gadgets which could make launching a commercial organisation less complex.

Selecting the right spot is step one. The are searching for for starts offevolved inside the Vehicles and Trucks region. Click the For Sale location as soon as your are seeking has been greater focused.

You must start through looking at the listing's snap shots. Craigslist pictures can be low-

decision, however they'll furthermore have some caution symptoms. For example, look beforehand to any symptoms of corrosion or harm. That applies to each the truck and the food trailer you're thinking about.

The VIN can be used to accumulate a Carfax file. This may additionally additionally contradict or help the records you're receiving from the seller.

Make every try and patronize your community agencies. Meeting in character notably lowers the danger of turning into a sufferer of fraud.

Find out why the man or woman offered a few element on Craigslist. You need if you need to decide the entire rate from the reaction.

Remember that dealers can be asking for more money than they think they'll accumulate. That indicates that at the same time as you meet in man or woman, there is continuously opportunity for a few haggling.

Finding a Food Truck via Professional Websites

You may additionally additionally moreover encompass a look for a food truck on precise net websites to your enterprise corporation technique. On specialized web websites, you could find out an remarkable vehicle if you understand what to search for. Websites devoted to meals truck manufacturers exist. They offer a variety of purchasing and leasing alternatives. Several web sites provide lists of truthful dealers; you could even find one for your u . S . A . By means of way of the use of their listing.

Some of those may be customizable for customers. Below is a list of sincere places to behavior business enterprise.

usedfoodtrucks.Com

This internet retailer offers a high-quality collection of food vehicles and trailers. Category and place are looking for choices. Your are searching out can be in addition narrowed down with the useful resource of fireplace suppression competencies and 365 days. This internet site furthermore has a list of food trucks damaged down with the useful resource of country. Food trailers have comparable listings.

This business corporation moreover sells a map of food vehicles which can be inside the marketplace. Click on the nation to view listings with expenses and snap shots.

Appetite Wandering

Roaming Hunger is a meals truck gateway of types. At this hooked up order, you could look for and reserve this form of gadgets for catering. You can discover one via manner of the use of their interactive map as properly. The meals trucks in this listing are to be had for sports activities along with weddings, charity abilties, and agency catering. They positioned up their menu objects directly to the internet web site from their kitchen. Customers can time table a catering event or place an order earlier the usage of a tab.

In addition, they offer masses of advertising and advertising services like influencer networking and emblem cognizance constructing.

acquiring a meals truck from a enterprise fleet

Numerous strategies may be used to start a food truck corporation. Numerous big businesses have opened workplaces in particular cities over the years. One of the numerous groups that has run one is Google Food Trucks. The big Internet agency operated a fleet from 2015 to 2017. Some particular names are McCain and AT&T.

Owning a vehicle is critical for businesses. This form of cellular restaurant is attractive to three folks that want to serve their employees and clients. This shape of vehicle is likewise used by others to deliver meals to emergency reaction humans. It's an additional desire to remember.

They present an exquisite possibility for branding. The method outlined above desires to be adhered to even as shopping for a meals truck from a employer fleet.

These additionally permit companies to take part in out of doors live performance events, gala's, and network gala's.

Examining Classified Advertisements

There are advertisements for meals cars available available on the market every nationally and domestically. It's vital to look for first rate photographs in each. Contact facts is likewise very crucial. Offering customers, a choice of phone numbers, email addresses, and postal addresses is brilliant.

A variety of markets must be blanketed by means of manner of manner of national commercials. This will assist you decide wherein the customers are. Additionally, think about promoting your labeled advertising and marketing on social media net sites like Facebook pages. Look for this service on one-of-a-kind social media structures as nicely.

Acquisitions from Specialized Manufacturers

What a few people need to rent to get into this market is a customized unit. You ought to pick a dependable producer to keep away from in addition anxiety. It is vital to realise your monetary fame and the equipment you want. It's critical to recognize in which you may be strolling and what shape of meals you will be serving.

Usually, a custom producer will ship a blueprint. Customers can regulate it after that. Usually, it takes the ones producers to a few months to complete an order.

Recall that a widespread food truck measures sixteen feet in duration and 7 ft in width. For your employer, a meals truck, food cart, or food trailer might be required.

Furthermore, you have to decide if it will run on diesel or gasoline. A diesel generator that is cellular may be the energy supply. Retractable awnings and vinyl wraps are only of the severa exceptional alternatives available.

Budget for brought talents like a difficulty-of-sale machine. Remember that you will be seeking to hassle in the price of food on a everyday foundation. And they're only a few of the alternatives that exist. This form of eating place is far greater popular.

Talking with Other Food Truck Operators

Speaking with other food truck operators is a few other notable approach to benefit statistics. A list of close by corporations that you can contact is supplied right here. A listing of towns and subjects to cover is furnished. Use the place are searching out to discover the fine places to begin.

Look for a house owner who is willing to talk about specifics, which include the association of the kitchen, among other matters. Find out about the fee and in addition capabilities of a propane tank. Talking with those human beings enables you recognize this meals industry. It is even viable to pick out the finest meal unit. Remember to invite approximately the capability for beginning a franchise for meals vehicles.

How Much Does It Cost to Purchase a Food Truck?

The kind of meals truck you desire to purchase will dictate the rate. Whether you choose out to buy a extremely-contemporary vehicle, purchase a used truck, or rent a meals truck will have an effect on the charge.

Some provide better competencies but are extra pricey.

Buying this sort of mobile eating place is wanted. Beyond what the bare eye can see, there can be extra to it.

Getting a New Truck to Start a Food Truck Business!

The fee variety for a emblem-new food truck is $100,000 to $a hundred 75,000. A new meals truck has benefits and downsides. The ability to pay for the item is the number one prerequisite. You want to be privy to all relevant recommendations, license requirements, and allows.

The new kitchen on a brand-new food truck is one perk. Along with the house device is mostly a entire producer guarantee. Compared to used domestic gadget, a new kitchen might require fewer maintenance over time. Furthermore, the home system require lots less protection.

How Much Does It Cost to Purchase a Used Food Truck?

An outstanding opportunity to a modern day vehicle is to buy a secondhand meals truck in case you lack the finances for one. Purchasing an older meals truck would possibly in all likelihood come for as little as $35,000. You can collect a decent buy for sort of fifty thousand bucks.

Chapter 7: Additional Start-Up Expenses For Restaurants To Consider

The buy of the auto isn't always the handiest price associated with the food truck. There are a number of exclusive topics to keep in mind to your organization. They moreover cover inspection and parking prices similarly to coverage and permits for Meals Company. Below is a summary of some of the capital goals for walking this form of company.

Parking charges in line with month may also range from $250 to $2,000. Naturally, this presupposes that you do now not have a number of region on which to park your food truck.

The charge of an occasion might in all likelihood variety from $500 to $1,000.

Kitchenware is, of path, the most essential requirement here. Sadly, there aren't many vans to be had for buy that have already got freight inner of them.

You also can moreover make use of custom designed automobile covers for marketing. There are masses of meals vans the use of round. Yours need to stand out and proudly show your business enterprise employer.

Building a client base starts with advertising and advertising and advertising and a internet site. Consider electronic mail marketing and advertising to your food truck business business enterprise as well. A strong social media presence may even assist draw clients to your booth sooner or later of specific pop-up sports activities.

One of your fee alternatives is probably a issue-of-sale device, which can be had for as little as $50 a month.

We have not even cited the price of the meal however. It will all rely upon how your truck is used. Napkins, utensils, plates, and comparable gadgets also are desired for this shape of meals truck. That can come at a monthly price of as much as $500. The degree of sturdy factor of the agency will decide how a high-quality deal the ones prices vary.

Which meals truck—new or used—is higher?

To many organisation proprietors, adding an extra unit is a wonderful idea. Despite the larger preliminary price, you won't have to pay for costly maintenance. Here are some blessings of purchasing a modern-day truck.

You can alter the ones to healthy the requirements of the humans you need to achieve.

A emblem-new vehicle will make you appearance immaculate.

Large upkeep and malfunctions do now not usually warrant right now hobby.

This type of cellular kitchen comes with actual warranties.

There are some bad components. For instance, the preliminary outlay is enormous. Additionally, customization takes a touch longer. There is a lengthier organized duration inside the starting.

There are blessings and disadvantages to shopping for a used truck. For instance, proprietors of food motors thing out that the residence device in the kitchen are already there. Some elements, like a serving window, are instantaneous. These merchandise are to begin with lots much less pricey. This way that you may maintain coins while you start a food truck. They may want to probably even have a issue-of-sale tool geared up.

Buying a used item has numerous terrible factors. These consist of:

These trucks aren't as durable as new ones.

It isn't always feasible to assure the history or placed on and tear.

Getting someone to position into effect the modifications may be hard.

The amount of money you have available up front will determine whether or not or no longer you buy a cutting-edge day or used unit.

What is the month-to-month charge of going for walks a meals truck?

Every month, this shape of organisation incurs charges. You need to set aside the subsequent sums of coins each month.

Step van and food truck proprietors are required to pay for the commissary parking areas they employ. For that, the month-to-month rate range is $1,00 to $15,000. More in a few regions, perhaps.

You might want to rent an area so that you can put together the food that you sell. The month-to-month apartment price of a commercial kitchen ranges from $500 to $1500. The not unusual monthly gas charge in your pickup and cooking is $600.

Maintenance and truck coverage typically price as a good buy as $4 hundred a month, even though they may range.

Are food motors a prudent investment?

This company has grown extensively whilst you don't forget that 2015, which makes it a exquisite place to invest. But you may additionally need so that it will finances for one-of-a-kind costs, like food, and characteristic a strong business plan. If you're a businessperson with out the price range to open a eating place, that may be a incredible place to start.

What is the earnings of food vehicles?

The median incomes range for this sort of agency owner is $50,000 to $ hundred,000. About 1/2 of of truck proprietors make as a minimum $2 hundred,000 a three hundred and sixty five days, constant with facts. Being a chef lowers the startup prices for this kind of company. That indicates better earnings.

Section Three

How to Draft a Business Plan for a Food Truck

The avenue food agency extended at an average each yr price of 7.Five percent amongst 2015 and 2020, and it end up valued greater than $1 billion within the US by myself. It's time to discover the way to start a profitable commercial enterprise! The first step is to put in writing the organisation technique!

Without the charge and danger of walking a bodily restaurant, a food truck is the proper area for individuals who want to end up first rate cooks to attempt out new recipes, assemble a following, or perhaps launch an internet business corporation. A Michelin-starred Street food cook dinner dinner in Singapore proves which you do now not need a massive kitchen with fifty sous cooks to build a reputation for brilliant, creativity, and deliciousness.

Food vans have become increasingly popular, so putting in maintain is as crucial as installing region your setup. A stable meals truck business plan places you in advance of the %

at the same time as the race starts offevolved.

How to write down down down a food truck marketing and marketing approach

Starting a road meals enterprise agency entails the same risks and disturbing conditions as special startup endeavors. However, there are sure problems that meals vehicles need to overcome earlier than you open the window and begin serving sandwiches (or tacos, or fish fry, or...).

You may additionally need to apply our accessible advertising approach template to write down down your thoughts as they come to you.

We'll stroll you thru every step of writing a food truck advertising and marketing method, from the govt. Summary to the monetary data, to make certain scrumptious fulfillment.

1. You must set up your government precis on a unmarried internet page.

You must write this portion of your advertising and marketing method remaining, despite the fact that it's far the primary one. As your government summary will incorporate all of the salient factors from the the rest of your marketing strategy, get matters organized first.

Remember who you are writing this for while you write it. If you're writing a advertising approach for your self, this synopsis may be brief and dirty and could allow you to preserve organized, brought about, and purpose targeted.

Do not overthink style or flare; as a substitute, deal with the most important elements of your advertising method. To create a list of the important responsibilities you need to complete in advance than serving Korean fried chook, you can also hire bullet factors.

If the goal of your advertising method is to benefit a economic corporation mortgage, then your authorities summary must highlight profitability, dependability, and your recognize-a way to make your food truck look like a nice element.

Emphasize the specific elements of your food issuer version, but additionally make an effort to reveal that you apprehend the issues of walking a small commercial business enterprise employer.

2. Write a summary of your business enterprise.

In this segment, you could provide an explanation for what makes your food truck a success and considered one of a type from others which may be currently strolling on the road.

During this segment, you may want to tell your target market why you're certified to run a profitable meals enterprise. Do you've got any previous culinary experience? Have you held manipulate of a enterprise pantry before? Do you already have a call for generating scrumptious meals? Depending on how desirable your concept is, banks may possibly help you, but your possibilities are better when you have enjoy.

Despite missing any formal training in cooking, Mikey and Natalie from Eats Amoré come from an extended line of proficient chefs. "Traditional dishes produced with sparkling additives are the cornerstone of Italian cooking, which Natalie learnt from her mom, an natural farmer. Her grandmother, an Italian close by from Naples, taught her a manner to cook dinner.

Workers

This segment must moreover outline your personal feature in the meals truck industrial business enterprise and the styles of employees you've got already had been given or should require hiring. Since food motors are small, you normally might not want a huge group on the street, but you can want to take into account hiring prep human beings, cleaners, and certainly one of a type personnel participants.

Objectives

The exceptional area to set dreams is within the company examine. Most food truck operators (and restaurateurs, for that consider) intention to repay most in their preliminary fees (licensing fees, insurance, belongings, food, net net sites, branding, and so forth.) within the first 12 months, despite the fact that this could extensively rely on your projected margins.

Obtaining a gap at a huge occasion, building a social media following, and locating honest parking spots to draw repeat commercial agency are a few special quick-time period desires.

Your largest capital outlay will in reality be the truck itself; even as starting a food truck is a good deal less costly than beginning a traditional eating place, the setup charges can though range from $50,000 to $a hundred seventy five,000, depending on what shape of food you ought to serve and the machine you will want. Ultimately, you can probably need to repay your food truck with each Shopify Capital or your very private price range.

3. Conduct a market evaluation

To characteristic your agency for success, it is important which you comprehend the marketplace in which it's going to characteristic.

Restrictions

Food vehicles are greater cell than ingesting locations, so that you could have greater freedom. However, as a part of your operating license, which generally costs $1,800, many groups nevertheless have recommendations on in which, at the same time as, and the way you may serve clients.

For instance, if you had been to begin a meals truck in Vancouver, you would find that there are various rules, like now not walking at night time time, avoiding certain neighborhoods, staying 100 meters an extended manner from real eating places, staying outdoor park limits, and loads of extra. You might also come across issues in case your high-quality customers live and artwork in a place or at a time at the equal time as you aren't capable of benefit them.

It's possible that a city's prison hints have not usually included meals automobiles, in which case you can need to clean the floor on your organisation-like Mikey and Natalie did. "We had only a few opportunities for places. In Kamloops, the zoning changed into terrible. Not many human beings gave us excessive first-rate interest. After lots to and fro, multiple council conferences, and emails exchanged with counselors, we have been capable to steer the metropolis to provide us with a pilot venture area in the middle of the town.

For extra records at the restrictions that your municipality imposes on meals truck operators, go to the net internet site on line of the community metropolis corridor. Additionally, get commenced early because of the reality it can take the time to accumulate a license, specifically in excessive-demand places.

nearby conditions

Every town is issue to sports that are not controlled via municipalities and could both help or keep off your employer. In Edmonton, you may probably best get the nice and comfortable, sunny climate required for an ice cream truck for 4 months of the twelve months, which can appreciably lessen income. In San Diego, alternatively, in which there are normally 266 days of daytime a yr, the same ice cream truck also can cause a sensation with lines extending throughout the block.

You must don't forget the following elements while estimating the type of days consistent with one year you'll be able to perform foot visitors inside the neighborhoods of your choice, demographics of the city's population, and the frequency of food truck occasions.

opposition

Finally, do not forget opposition. Are there many food trucks on your town or at the parking spot you need to apply? Is there a flourishing restaurant enterprise that is subsidized through owners who're afraid meals vans will take their agency? It can be difficult to discover clients or a parking spot if there can be too much opposition. If it is too little, you may find out that there may be a notable reason no character runs meals vehicles.

four. Explain the goods or offerings you provide.

In this segment, you can have the possibility to proportion your revolutionary culinary ideas. However, have in mind that there are limitations and problems regarding the food that leaves your truck.

Food should be clean to devour on numerous surfaces without spilling over a CEO's Brooks Brothers blouse, this shape of bench, a sidewalk, or a packed concert.

Keep it clean: with restricted place, group of workers, device, and storage, it can be difficult or no longer viable to offer a large, complex menu, irrespective of the truth that you may be able to make modern-day man or woman products.

A prolonged menu can be daunting or time-eating for the ones looking to location a short order at some point of their lunch damage.

Attempt to fill a need for your community. If a variety of pizza vendors are round however no Thai eateries, make som tam in choice to a margherita pie. Or, for instance, in case you live in an area in which several meals vans are selling inferior burgers, your very top notch model might likely nook the market. The pricing of your merchandise may additionally set them aside.

Look into what sort of meals truck scene already exists on your region to get an idea of what should artwork. Natalie explains, "We went to Vancouver in particular to speak to as many owners as we may additionally need to approximately what is taking area and what obstacles you come across. We furthermore went to Portland and Seattle, in which severa of those vehicles gave us useful recommendation.

Here, it might be clever to bear in mind opportunity sales streams, such net income of merchandise like spice packs, baked gadgets, and bottled sauces. In times while gala's aren't taking area, as inside the course of the gradual wintry climate months, or perhaps inside the occasion of a worldwide epidemic, on line sales want to show to be quite beneficial.

Eats Amoré has determined that on line profits and catering reservations are increasingly more important to its economic trendy typical performance thru its Shopify website. "It's gotten so busy that we've to show it on and stale," Mikey says.

If you purchase a subscription from our on line maintain, you will get preserve of three deliveries of mystery ravioli to your private home each weeks.

When it got here to reading a way to conduct net earnings, Mikey acknowledges that he modified into pretty inexperienced. "I'm however studying lots," he remarks.

"And income are developing considerably irrespective of the minimum studying I've finished in small increments. It no longer handiest prolonged our income however additionally decreased the quantity of time I had to spend speaking with humans. Because extra people call you and need to hire you [for catering], and also you get masses fewer tire kickers regardless of the whole thing of your information is on the internet internet site."

Chapter 8: The Communications Plan For A Brand

The number one elements that enchantment to functionality clients from the road are parking and truck look, so start thru offering an in depth description of every. Next, provide a cause behind how you recommend using conventional advertising and marketing strategies, especially social media, to get your industrial enterprise in front of extra people than surely pedestrians.

Sugar & Spoon in Seattle has completed a terrific venture of coordinating the advent and experience of its food, vehicles, net web page, and extremely good Instagram feed to beautify its logo identity anywhere clients may come upon it.

Following you on Instagram, Twitter, and/or Face book is a outstanding manner to allow human beings recognize in which you park on specific days. Social media is the great area to inform your lover's approximately new menu gadgets. If you want to exhibit your food as a terrific deal as possible, take into account to take brilliant pics.

We discussed how your menu must occupy a spot beneath the Products and Services region, whether or not or no longer or not it's miles in phrases of high-quality, charge, or delicacies fashion. In this section, you need to very well supply an purpose of ways you want to talk the ones differentiators for your customers. Your advertising and marketing and marketing and advertising and marketing technique ought to think about how your services and products stand pleased with the opposition.

Online buying

In relation to generation, that is a extraordinary time to have a test the opportunity that your clients gets in contact with you thru laptops and cellular telephones.

You may need to offer online ordering with delivery or pickup the use of 1/3-birthday celebration services like DoorDash, Skip the Dishes, Uber Eats, or any huge variety of different apps desired in particular markets across the area; just make certain to discover which app most local eating places and delivery services use.

If you do not ought to wait in line, you may be able to get greater completed in an afternoon, that's first-rate information for compelled-out, ravenous office personnel.

When

The start date is a much less obvious a part of your advertising plan. If you desire to open within the summer season, you can most probable be too busy to commit a good deal time to growing your on line presence and brand identity, however your cash glide will truly be massive.

If you live somewhere with extremely good winter climate, you might want to don't forget taking a few time without work over the wintry weather. However, starting later inside the 12 months will give you time to turn out to be organized and acclimate to the tempo of running a meals truck, no matter the fact that it approach fewer earnings.

"We didn't without a doubt change proper right into a three hundred and sixty 5 days-round business company agency until we created our Shopify account last wintry weather," Mikey says. "Working thru the wintry climate have come to be one in all the largest mistakes we made in our first yr's marketing approach," he says. However, I left out to say that Kamloops citizens are especially truthful-weathered and accustomed to wonderful climate. So, they may be announcing, "No, we are out of right here," after feeling a touch little bit of the cold.

7. Create a logistics and operations plan.

In this segment, you will want to dive right into the every day operations of your meals truck.

supply chain

You need substances to promote food, however in on the way to you discover them? Let's have a look at your options.

For instance, Sysco Restaurant Wholesalers is a sincere and cheap enterprise agency.

Cons: Keeping cumbersome boxed items on your truck may be tough.

LARGE-SAVING CLUB

Costco Advantages, as an example: It's available to keep on every occasion you want.

Cons: Prices can be greater than what eating place wholesalers fee.

MARKET LOCATIONS

Local greengrocers, forte markets, and Trader Joe's are a few examples.

Smaller bundle deal sizes and the broadest preference of factors—including place of understanding, herbal, and close by additives—are blessings.

Cons: Pricey.

Consider your menu: when you have a fixed menu of meal alternatives, will you be able to continuously collect the same devices at some degree inside the year? If your menu modifications frequently, will you've got got the time to deliver sparkling materials on a regular foundation? Many meals truck operators use a combination of carriers to achieve their goals. Look at what is to be had on your area that suits interior your menu and your price range.

Mikey has determined out that their truck's allure stems in component from the herbal and domestically sourced meals they use.

Establishment

Your truck is your facility, so count on cautiously about the kind of car you need to get.

To placed it every other manner, Mikey says, "We placed a deal in this HandyDART bus and spent the primary a part of 2013 turning it proper into a food truck. We found masses. Unlike a massive stainless truck, the automobile's fiberglass production wasn't suitable, but we made it paintings. Retrofitting a much much much less-than-excellent automobile may be an preference for you, or you can want to buy a vehicle that grow to be constructed to be a meals truck.

This element describes the physical requirements for the device for your industrial organisation, which incorporates: specialised cooking machine, tires, brakes, batteries, and gasoline (cooking and engine). However, you could want your facilities for plenty greater than surely setting four wheels on the floor.

Furthermore, you have to plan for the charge and logistics involved in having exceptional meals education obligations—like lowering vegetables, making soups, baking bread, or making geared up one-of-a-kind components—finished in an off-net web page commissary kitchen after profits hours in choice to inside the food truck or at your private home to make sure meals safety.

Find out if there can be room for added component storage at the commissary cooking vicinity.

Potential for manufacturing

How lengthy does it usually take to put together one among your menu gadgets? This is an vital hobby that would restrict the sort of customers you can serve every day. Moreover, a meals truck can possibly pleasant keep a restrained quantity of employees, no matter what number of people are anticipating food; this isn't always the case with traditional restaurants, that could lease greater frame of people at the same time as enterprise is specifically strong.

More exertions is going into it than maximum humans recognize, so make sure to account for the way loads paintings you could whole on your non-public. "I go home and do dishes for 2 hours," gives Mikey. How do you intend to address versions in call for and pace in some unspecified time inside the future of the course of an afternoon, week, month, or three hundred and sixty five days?

Delivery

If you propose to promote products on-line, you can want to recollect delivery. Luckily, transport can be done correctly and cost effectively.

8. Make your monetary plan public.

Like most agencies, yours will in all likelihood succeed or fail based totally on the excellent of your monetary plan. You need to recognise how a exquisite deal cash is coming in, going out, and how the ones numbers are expected to alternate within the future, so make sure to carefully take a look at your capability stability sheet to really recognize how prices and profits can have an impact on your enterprise.

Profit margin

Though the meals truck organisation model can constrain your revenues, fortunately, a food truck's preliminary charges are significantly lower than those of a normal restaurant, so your damage-even difficulty might in all likelihood come a good buy quicker.

You probably may not be able to get alcohol because most governments forbid meals trucks from selling alcohol and regular eating locations typically estimate a 30 percent take benefit of alcohol sales; food vehicles, however, may additionally additionally anticipate a median income of about eight%, indicating that they will be quantity companies that ought to feature rapid to service huge numbers of customers to turn a earnings.

Menu pricing is critical to your monetary plan when you recollect that, relying on in which you set up keep, it could be hard to rate $25 for a food truck cheeseburger, no matter how masses it expenses to fabricate. In addition, clients may additionally additionally moreover apprehend a most charge for certain dishes, together with hamburgers.

Food vans can not carry a whole lot of products, so you'll want to sell and restock extra often than a brick-and-mortar restaurant. You additionally want to provide an reason at the back of your cash go together with the waft situation.

Additional fees

If you have body of employees, this is moreover the segment in which you need to fee variety for particular costs like personnel salaries, protection, and licensing. You must also do not forget that, in case you do not plan to recruit help, in case you need to additionally decrease your sales, you probable can not paintings 16 hours a day, seven days every week.

Write that commercial enterprise method right away.

Now that you've had a threat to expect via how your food truck aspirations have to impact it, it's time to sit down down and compose your meals truck marketing strategy.

Ideas for Food Truck Themes and Illustrations for Your Novel Idea

Although many agree with food trucks are a passing style, they look like proper right here to stay. These mobile eateries have lengthy past an extended manner from turning in ice cream and warm puppies to in recent times imparting gourmet cupcakes, sandwiches, and ethnic fusion avenue meals. If you may increase a a success concept and menu, you may be able to release a food truck specialization. The menus at the ones cell eating places will evolve as they grow. Food automobiles are a high-quality way to introduce the overall public in your culinary requirements due to the fact they'll be visible at weddings, personal activities, and one-of-a-kind activities and feature low initial costs.

Grilled

Barbecue is a exceptional concept as it combines excessive appeal with fairly priced delicacies. Carnivore BBQ, located in Washington, D.C., blends the tremendous factors of Texas-fashion fish fry with domestically grown factors and recyclable packaging. An extra advantage? The great, smokey fragrance emanating out of your truck is a shape of guerilla marketing during way of itself.

Cupcakes

This culinary fashion has tested to be resilient. Gourmet cupcakes may be elegantly or clearly displayed. Sassi Cakes in Buffalo, New York offers a full-size form of gourmand cupcakes, including alcoholic liquids like sangria and margarita. They also supply cupcakes within a 50-mile radius and provide catering offerings to enhance their earnings margin.

blending of numerous ethnic organizations

Combining one or extra ethnic cuisines results in some superb thoughts. Nowadays, instances of ethnic fusion are Korean barbecue and Vietnamese cuisine. A lot of conventional Filipino meals are given a contemporary-day makeover at Guerrilla Street Food in St. Louis, Missouri. One such delicacy is the Sisig Taco, which incorporates braised and sautéed pig belly, tongue, and ears. Food automobiles normally inspire attempting some issue new.

Paninis

Paninis are gourmand-fashion sandwiches. They provide some of ingesting alternatives with very little machine (a panini presses or). They are best for folks that are consuming lunch, and additionally they make a exceptional after-paintings snack. Bikini Panini, positioned in Richmond, Virginia, sells paninis and specific Mediterranean-fashion meals.

Chapter 9: Local And Herbal Food

Locally produced and natural meals ought to not want to be boring. As it takes area, the flavors are frequently notably advanced to the ones of professionally cultivated meals. A meals truck can also feature itself as a sustainable organisation through using providing without a doubt to be had, locally sourced meat and vegetables. Would you want to keep? Upgrade to a hybrid or biodiesel engine in vicinity of your modern one.

European alternatives

The Old World is coming again through food vehicles. Along with bratwurst (obviously), paprika bird, Austrian goulash, and bratwurst, The Bratwurst King furthermore offers domestic made pastries and strudel. Promote the concept of culinary excursion as lots as you can. You're advertising and marketing it.

Local American Cuisine

Red Hook Lobster Pound food truck offers you Maine lobster to New York City. The food truck offers a number of true New England staples, together with clam chowder and lobster rolls. There are automobiles which can be appropriate for poutine, tacos, gumbo, and similarly. Provide an tremendous or service that human beings aren't probable to find out close by.

Waffles Waffle vans provide a desire of waffles, including greater cutting-edge kinds with blueberries and lemon cream cheese filling and traditional versions with butter and maple syrup. Like paninis or tacos, this concept can be served almost any time of day and might be further well-preferred for breakfast as it might be at 3 inside the morning. You can also locate some thing at Waffle Crush in Phoenix, Arizona, to in shape each mood and time of day.

burgers

Burgers may be made definitely or tastefully and are continuously a crowd desired. Not brilliant are burgers one of the most ate up meals, however they also sell properly time and time over again. There are too a whole lot of those trucks to rely. Consider inclusive of a version from every other type on our listing to make your burger truck precise.

pastries crafted from ice.

An ice cream truck, a rustic full-size icon, and the actual meals truck problem is a clean canvas, so allow your creativity run wild. You can serve velvety Italian gelato along conventional American ice cream flavors like peanut butter fudge or rocky avenue. Better even though, think about home made gelato popsicles. More enterprising ice cream truck owners first-class sell their merchandise at some level mainly instances of the 12 months, changing the truck or renting it out actually.

There are meals trucks with concern subjects and types galore. There are new traits each day. How will yours seem like?

The Commercial Gear Needed for a Food Truck

A new eating place's business kitchen is set up similarly to how a food truck is. It desires to be prepared, cooled, saved, and served in taken into consideration one among a kind regions. As a meals truck's kitchen is generally a good buy smaller than a restaurant's, you need to make the maximum of every rectangular inch this is available. Your food truck's format is probably closely inspired through its menu; will you be producing huge quantities of sandwiches or wraps off-internet site on line, or in-house? (consisting of pizza or fried cuisine). It is critical that your food truck conforms to all relevant neighborhood and kingdom fitness and safety criminal suggestions, no matter the form of delicacies it plans to serve.

areas for purchasing prepared and storing food trucks.

Enclosed cabinets or cabinets are high-quality for storing non-perishables like paper items and dry gadgets. Make sure cupboard doors are near firmly before you pressure. Built-in prep counter tops are the best; they need to be built of a meals-regular material, like stainless-steel (no wooden counters, please). Just as in a eating place kitchen, maintain a consistent vicinity amongst meals, serving utensils, and cleansing substances.

Stoves, grills, and refrigeration for meals motors

All freezers, fridges, and coolers need to be secured to the ground for safety. There need to moreover be appropriate air flow and electric powered shops. This function is shared thru deep fats fryers, ovens, and enterprise barbecues. Furthermore, stovetops and barbecues may also furthermore need hoods with fanatics and sprinkler structures that are well vented to the out of doors.

Food truck carrier window

To serve purchasers, your meals truck have to have at the least one large window. You can save condiments, disposable cutlery, and napkins on an outdoor counter. An awning over the window is a smart buy, come rain or shine.

Food truck safety and health

For your truck to be certified or allowed to carry out as a food truck, it must skip a fire and protection inspection. The neighborhood ordinances will dictate the specifics of the inspection. Fire alarms, sprinkler systems, extinguishers, and foodHowever, secure surfaces for the partitions and flooring are critical. Make certain to talk along side your neighborhood licensing department earlier than deciding on the very last format for your meals truck.

This is a preference made with the beneficial resource of positive cellular kitchen operators. They have lots of location to prepare and keep meals because of this. If you recommend to utilize your private home kitchen to put together meals for your food truck, it must be inspected and updated thru the use of your state's nearby health administrative center. To positioned it it seems that evidently, cooking food at domestic and then promoting it from a meals truck is a criminal offense.

Chapter 10: The Food Truck Industry

1.1: The upward thrust of the meals truck phenomenon

The meals truck phenomenon represents a dynamic and innovative shift inside the culinary panorama, remodeling the manner human beings enjoy and eat meals. This movement has gained large momentum over the last decade, reshaping town consuming scenes and difficult traditional notions of restaurant eating. Several factors have contributed to the rise of the meals truck phenomenon.

1. Entrepreneurial Spirit and Lower Entry Barriers: The meals truck enterprise is characterised with the useful useful resource of its entrepreneurial spirit, attracting cooks

and cooks keen to exhibit their culinary competencies without the massive monetary investment required for a brick-andmortar restaurant. The decrease get admission to boundaries has allowed a various kind of people to go into the food enterprise and test with specific and place of hobby cuisines.

2. Flexibility and Mobility: One of the defining talents of meals trucks is their mobility. They can installation keep in diverse locations for the duration of the day, catering to unique audiences and responding to converting client dreams. This flexibility lets in meals truck proprietors to participate in activities, festivals, and markets, engaging in a broader customer base compared to conventional eating places.

3. Innovative Cuisine and Fusion Trends: Food vehicles are mentioned for their present day and often experimental technique to cuisine. Many food vehicles specialize in fusion cuisine, mixing culinary traditions from unique cultures to create precise and exciting

flavor mixtures. This creativity has resonated with customers looking for novel and Instagram-surely worth consuming reports.

four. Social Media and Digital Marketing: Social media structures, along side Instagram, Twitter, and Facebook, have done a pivotal characteristic in the fulfillment of food motors. These systems provide a fee-powerful manner for meals truck proprietors to market their services, percentage their locations in actual-time, and interact with their client base. The visually appealing nature of food truck delicacies makes it quite shareable, contributing to the enterprise's popularity on social media.

5. Changing Consumer Preferences: Modern consumers an increasing number of charge comfort, range, and authenticity. Food trucks align with the ones alternatives with the resource of providing short and available food, severa menu options, and an intimate, custom designed connection among the client and the chef. Many clients recognize the

transparency and authenticity of looking their food being prepared right within the the the front of them.

6. Supportive Regulatory Environment: In many cities, guidelines and attitudes towards food trucks have advanced to aid the enterprise's growth. Some municipalities have created exact regions for food vehicles, streamlined allowing techniques, and implemented food protection requirements to make sure the legitimacy and incredible of cell culinary operations.

7. Cultural and Economic Impact: The food truck phenomenon has emerge as extra than best a culinary fashion; it has become a cultural and monetary pressure. Food cars make contributions to the vibrancy of metropolis spaces, supporting community economies and developing a sense of community. Additionally, they have come to be incubators for emerging culinary abilities, permitting chefs to test, refine their offerings,

and in all likelihood transition to permanent eating place ventures

The upward thrust of the meals truck phenomenon displays a confluence of things, together with entrepreneurship, mobility, culinary innovation, virtual advertising, changing customer alternatives, regulatory help, and cultural impact. As this fashion maintains to adapt, it's miles probable that meals motors will stay a dynamic and important part of the modern-day-day culinary panorama.

Benefits of Operating a Food Truck:

1. Lower Initial Investment: One of the number one blessings of beginning a food truck organization is the appreciably decrease initial funding as compared to a conventional brickand-mortar restaurant. Entrepreneurs can input the food company with a smaller price range, making it a more available opportunity for those with restricted capital.

2. Mobility and Flexibility: Food cars are cellular, permitting owners to gain special locations and cater to diverse audiences. This mobility offers flexibility to take part in activities, gala's, and excessive-site visitors regions, optimizing earnings and exposure.

three. Direct Customer Interaction: Food trucks provide a completely unique possibility for direct interplay among chefs or owners and customers. This personal connection can help build a committed purchaser base, acquire instant comments, and alter the menu primarily based absolutely mostly on purchaser options.

four. Innovative Culinary Expression: Operating a meals truck lets in chefs to check with modern and revolutionary culinary principles. The constrained location encourages common performance and specialization, fostering unique and regularly fashion-putting menu gadgets.

five. Social Media Marketing: The visually attractive nature of meals truck cuisine makes it relatively shareable on social media systems. Owners can leverage the ones systems for fee-effective advertising, enticing with their goal marketplace, and saying their locations in real-time.

6. Adaptability to Trends: Food vehicles can rapid adapt to rising meals dispositions and customer alternatives. This agility permits owners to stay competitive and applicable, adjusting their menu and services based definitely totally on converting culinary and dietary dispositions.

7. Lower Overhead Costs: Compared to traditional ingesting places, meals vehicles generally have lower overhead fees. Expenses associated with utilities, rent, and protection are generally reduced, contributing to a in all likelihood better income margin.

Challenges of Operating a Food Truck:

1. Limited Space and Storage: The compact duration of food vehicles may be a first-rate undertaking. Limited kitchen and garage

region also can moreover restriction the shape of menu objects and require careful inventory manage.

2. Weather Dependence: Food truck operations are intently stimulated thru weather conditions. Adverse climate, together with rain or excessive warmth, can effect profits and make it hard to perform, especially in out of doors places.

three. Permitting and Regulations: Navigating the complex internet of allows, licenses, and fitness regulations may be a time-consuming and bureaucratic method. Compliance with close by policies is vital and may variety from one location to three different.

4. Equipment Reliability: The reliance on mobile cooking gadget approach that breakdowns or malfunctions can disrupt operations. Regular protection and having backup plans in area are crucial to lessen downtime.

5. Competition and Saturation: As the meals truck agency continues to expand, opposition in certain Finding

markets can become intense.

unique selling factors and differentiating from competition can be hard, particularly in areas with a high awareness of food motors.

6. Limited Operating Hours: Food motors frequently have constrained strolling hours, in particular inside the occasion that they attention on lunch or overdue-night time crowds. This constraint can also restriction income capability in assessment to consuming places that would perform in the path of the day.

7. Parking Challenges: Finding suitable and crook parking regions can be a persistent challenge. Some places may additionally additionally have strict guidelines, and competition for top parking spots in famous regions can be fierce.

eight. Seasonal Fluctuations: Seasonal modifications can notably impact business. For instance, outside locations also can see decreased foot net site visitors all through much less heat months, leading to fluctuations in sales.

While strolling a meals truck offers diverse advantages, entrepreneurs need to navigate those disturbing situations to construct a a hit and sustainable business enterprise. Adaptability, powerful advertising, and a keen know-how of community suggestions are important for overcoming the hurdles of the meals truck enterprise corporation.

Trends and improvements in the food truck business enterprise agency

Culinary Fusion:

Many food motors are experimenting with fusion cuisine, combining wonderful culinary traditions to create unique and interesting flavor profiles. This lets in for a diverse menu that appeals to a considerable sort of tastes.

Healthy and Sustainable Options:

With the growing interest on health and sustainability, meals trucks are incorporating extra plant-based totally and domestically sourced components into their menus. This style aligns with the growing demand for extra wholesome food choices.

Technology Integration:

Food automobiles are leveraging generation to streamline operations and beautify the client enjoy. Mobile apps for ordering, cashless price options, and social media advertising and marketing and marketing have emerge as preferred practices.

Specialized Diets:

Food trucks are catering to specialised diets which include gluten-free, keto, vegan, and others. This lets in them to tap into place of interest markets and cater to a broader purchaser base.

Gourmet Offerings:

The notion of food automobiles as carriers of short and reasonably-priced eats is converting. Many food truck owners are specializing in connoisseur offerings, providing superb dishes that rival the ones decided in traditional consuming locations.

Branding and Unique Themes:

Successful meals vehicles often have a sturdy logo identity and a very unique subject. This may also need to encompass eyecatching snap shots, memorable names, and a constant seen presence on social media systems.

Data Analytics:

Some food vehicles are the usage of statistics analytics to recognize purchaser choices, song sales, and optimize their menus. This data permits them make information-pushed choices to beautify overall performance and profitability.

Alcohol Pairings:

To decorate the general ingesting experience, a few meals cars are taking part with nearby breweries or wineries to provide alcohol pairings with their dishes. This creates a extra sophisticated and exciting experience for clients.

Community Engagement:

Successful meals trucks often have interaction with their nearby groups via activities, partnerships, and social media. Building a devoted customer base is critical for sustained achievement inside the aggressive meals truck company.

Pop-Up Collaborations:

Food trucks are more and more participating with exclusive corporations or cooks for pop-up sports. This allows them to provide particular menu items and gain new audiences.

Dessert and Specialty Items:

Some meals automobiles cognizance on desserts or unique gadgets, catering to clients with a candy tooth or those looking for a few element splendid from the same old savory options.

Innovative Marketing Strategies:

Beyond social media, food motors are exploring modern advertising strategies which encompass influencer collaborations, interactive promotions, or maybe participation in meals festivals to boom visibility and attraction to customers.

As the food truck industry keeps to develop and adapt to changing patron alternatives, new tendencies and upgrades will possibly emerge. Entrepreneurs in this region have to live adaptable and open to embracing new thoughts to live in advance in this dynamic market.

Chapter 11: Market Research And Concept Development

2.1: Identifying your purpose market

An vital first step in any business commercial enterprise business enterprise planning method is figuring out your target market. Knowing who your customers are will assist you customise your services in phrases of products, offerings, and advertising and advertising and advertising to in shape their requirements and tastes. Here's a comprehensive how-to manual for determining your purpose marketplace:

1. Market Research:

Demographics: Start through amassing demographic information about capability customers. This consists of age, gender, income degree, training, career, and vicinity. This records enables create a critical profile of your target marketplace.

Psychographics: Dig deeper into the way of life, values, pursuits, and behaviors of your capability clients. This information provides insights into their motivations and purchasing picks.

Market Size: Determine the general length of your aim market. Understanding the capacity amount of customers lets in you to assess the agency possibility and market call for.

2. Customer Surveys and Feedback:

Conduct surveys and gather remarks out of your gift customers or a sample of your target market. Ask about their options, pain elements, and what affects their searching for selections. This firsthand facts is beneficial for refining your reason market.

three. Competitor Analysis:

Analyze your competition and choose out who they are concentrated on. Look for gaps or underserved segments that you can tap into. Differentiating your product or service may be less complex in case you discover a gap marketplace that isn't always efficiently addressed.

4. Social Media Insights:

Utilize social media analytics to recognize the demographics and behaviors of your fanatics or capability audience. Platforms like Facebook, Instagram, and Twitter offer insights into the age, vicinity, and hobbies of your intention market.

5. Google Analytics and Website Data:

If you've got a net net web page, examine the statistics the use of gear like Google Analytics. Understand wherein your net site internet site on-line visitors is coming from, which pages are well-known, and demographic facts about your on line visitors.

6. Industry Reports and Studies:

Explore organisation reviews and studies related to your enterprise. These documents often provide treasured facts on market trends, consumer behaviors, and the overall landscape. Government guides, change associations, and market research businesses may be suitable property.

7. Focus Groups:

Organize hobby agencies to acquire qualitative statistics. This includes bringing collectively a small agency of humans to speak about their mind, feelings, and perceptions approximately your products or services. This can offer rich insights into purchaser attitudes.

eight. Networking and Outreach:

To meet viable customers, go to alternate famous, enterprise gatherings, and networking sports. Talk to humans, make inquiries, and be aware of folks that unique hobby in what you want to provide.

9. Review Your Existing Customer Base:

Examine your gift customers. Determine the tendencies that your most profitable and devoted clients have in commonplace. This facts will let you in figuring out comparable human beings or companies.

10. Adaptability and Refinement:

Understand that your cause marketplace may additionally additionally evolve over time. Stay adaptable and be open to refining your target marketplace based on converting market situations, company developments, or shifts in consumer conduct.

11. Create Customer Personas:

Using the data acquired, create complete patron personas. These fictional characters constitute your ideal customers and help in visualizing and know-how their dreams, opportunities, and behaviors.

12. Test and Iterate:

Implement your strategies with a focused method and check the outcomes. If wished, be organized to iterate and refine your goal marketplace based absolutely totally on actual-worldwide comments and data.

By making an investment time and effort into identifying your goal marketplace, you lay a strong foundation for the success of your industrial enterprise. This way no longer excellent permits you tailor your services and products however moreover permits you to create greater effective advertising and marketing techniques that resonate along facet your target market.

2.2: Analyzing the competition

Analyzing the competition is a crucial detail of strategic making plans for any business organization. It includes comparing the strengths and weaknesses of opposition to apprehend opportunities and threats inside the market. This manner gives valuable insights which could assist a company make knowledgeable picks, refine its method, and benefit a aggressive benefit. Here's an in depth breakdown of the manner to efficiently look at the opposition:

1. Identify Competitors:

Direct Competitors: Businesses that cater to the identical motive marketplace with similar goods or services.

Indirect Competitors: Those presenting alternatives that satisfy the equal want or serve a similar reason.

Future Competitors: Emerging businesses or capability entrants into the marketplace.

2. Gather Information:

Company Background: Understand the history, assignment, values, and modern dreams of every competitor.

Products/Services: Analyze the variety, amazing, skills, and pricing in their services.

Market Share: Determine the marketplace percent of every competitor and the way it has modified over time.

Financials: Review financial statements, sales trends, and profitability.

Customer Base: Identify the target market and the techniques used to attract and maintain customers.

Distribution Channels: Evaluate how products or services are brought to clients.

Marketing and Branding: Examine their advertising and advertising and marketing and advertising techniques, messaging, and emblem positioning.

SWOT Analysis: Conduct a SWOT assessment for every competitor (Strengths, Weaknesses, Opportunities, Threats).

three. Benchmarking:

Compare Performance: Benchmark your personal usual overall performance in opposition to competition in key areas inclusive of income, marketplace percent, and client delight.

Best Practices: Identify organization fine practices and study how properly your competition adhere to them.

4. Competitive Positioning:

Unique Selling Proposition (USP): Determine the particular components that set your opposition apart.

Price Positioning: Understand their pricing strategy and the manner it compares to yours.

Product Differentiation: Analyze abilties, satisfactory, and innovation to pick out out elements of differentiation.

Brand Perception: Assess how clients understand competitor manufacturers in assessment to yours.

5. Market Trends:

Industry Analysis: Understand broader organisation tendencies, technological enhancements, and regulatory changes.

Customer Preferences: Identify shifts in client options and conduct.

Innovation: Evaluate competition' determination to innovation and their success in adopting new generation.

6. Risk Assessment:

External Risks: Identify outdoor elements that would effect competition (financial situations, regulatory adjustments, and so forth.).

Internal Risks: Assess internal vulnerabilities, such as manipulate issues or economic instability.

7. Customer Feedback:

Reviews and Testimonials: Analyze consumer reviews and testimonials for insights into competition' strengths and weaknesses.

Customer Surveys: Conduct surveys or test present ones to understand client pride with opposition.

8. Adaptation and Strategy Formulation:

Strategic Response: Develop techniques to counter or capitalize at the identified strengths and weaknesses of competition.

Continuous Monitoring: Regularly replace your evaluation to evolve to changes in the competitive panorama.

9. Collaboration Opportunities:

Partnerships or Alliances: Identify capability collaboration possibilities that can advantage both your enterprise and opposition.

10. Ethical Considerations:

Compliance and Ethics: Ensure your assessment and reaction adhere to ethical requirements and prison worries.

By systematically analyzing the opposition, corporations could make knowledgeable choices, beautify their competitive gain, and feature themselves for long-time period fulfillment in the market. Regularly updating this analysis is critical, given the dynamic nature of markets and industries.

2.Three: Developing a completely unique meals truck concept

Developing a totally unique meals truck concept includes a aggregate of creativity, market studies, and a deep records of your goal market. Here's an in depth guide on a way to cross approximately developing a specific and successful meals truck idea:

1. Market Research:

Identify Trends: Stay informed about modern-day food and culinary inclinations. Understand what's popular amongst your goal demographic.

Local Preferences: Take into consideration the culinary scene and customs to your region. Find any holes or unfulfilled desires inside the market.

Competitor Analysis: Look at cutting-edge eateries and food motors to find out a super area of interest and prevent duplication.

2. Define Your Niche:

Specialization: Decide on a selected delicacies, issue matter, or culinary attention that devices you apart.

Unique Selling Proposition (USP): Determine what's going to make your food truck stand out. It may be a signature dish, a completely unique cooking technique, or a topic that resonates collectively with your target market.

3. Create a Memorable Brand:

Brand Identity: Develop a strong and fantastic emblem identity, which includes a catchy name, emblem, and color scheme.

Storytelling: Craft a compelling story or problem depend that aligns collectively collectively along with your concept. This can create an emotional reference to customers.

four. Menu Innovation:

Signature Dishes: Create a few standout dishes that reflect your concept and go away an extended-lasting have an impact on.

Flexibility: Keep the menu easy but bendy. Consider dietary rules and provide customization alternatives.

Seasonal Offerings: Introduce seasonal or limited-time services to preserve the menu smooth and exciting.

5. Quality Ingredients and Preparation:

Source Locally: Whenever viable, use locally sourced and sparkling additives. This not pleasant lets in community companies but additionally gives authenticity on your concept.

Emphasize Quality: Focus on delivering terrific food continuously. Attention to detail in steerage and presentation can increase your meals truck's reputation.

6. Innovative Marketing:

Social Media Presence: Use social media web sites to unfold the word. Post in the again of-thescenes pix, provide menu modifications, and have interaction together at the side of your intention marketplace.

Food Photography: For use in advertisements and social media posts, spend money on top notch meals photographs

Events and Collaborations: To boost exposure, participate in network gatherings, paintings with unique agencies, and offer a hand with charitable endeavors.

7. Operational Efficiency:

Streamlined Operations: Design an green and well-organized kitchen format to optimize workflow.

Technology Integration: Consider the usage of era for order-taking, payments, and consumer engagement to enhance the general purchaser experience.

eight. Customer Feedback and Adaptation:

Collect Feedback: Actively are looking for for comments from clients to understand their selections and make critical adjustments.

Adapt to Trends: Stay flexible and be willing to evolve your concept based totally definitely mostly on changing tendencies and client feedback.

9. Compliance and Licensing:

Health and Safety Standards: Ensure that your meals truck meets all fitness and safety requirements. Obtain the essential licenses and lets in.

Local Regulations: Familiarize your self with community guidelines governing food vehicles, parking, and operation.

10. Community Engagement:

Build Relationships: Engage with the local community. Build relationships with customers, other food agencies, and groups inside the place.

www.ingramcontent.com/pod-product-compliance
Lightning Source LLC
Chambersburg PA
CBHW072157070526
44585CB00015B/1182